# NINJUTSU

An internationally recognized authority on Asian
martial arts, **Donn F. Draeger** was the first
non-Japanese to compete in the All-Japan High
Rank Holder's Judo Tournament at the Kodokan.
He has trained numerous Japanese and non-
Japanese in martial arts, many of whom have
gone on to become national, world, and Olympic
champions.

# NINJUTSU

## The Art of Invisibility

### Japan's Feudal-Age Espionage and Assassination Methods

By

## Donn F. Draeger

TUTTLE PUBLISHING
Tokyo • Rutland, Vermont • Singapore

First published in 1989 by Tuttle Publishing, an imprint of Periplus Editions (HK) Ltd., with editorial offices at 364 Innovation Drive, North Clarendon, Vermont 05759.

Library of Congress Catalog Card Number: 89-50021

ISBN: 0-8048-1597-6

Distributed by:

**North America, Latin America, and Europe**
Tuttle Publishing
364 Innovation Drive
North Clarendon, VT 05759-9436
Tel: (802) 773-8930
Fax: (802) 773-6993
Email: info@tuttlepublishing.com
Web site: www.tuttlepublishing.com

**Asia Pacific**
Berkeley Books Pte. Ltd.
130 Joo Seng Road
#06-01/03 Olivine Building
Singapore 368357
Tel: (65) 6280-1330
Fax: (65) 6280-6290
Email: inquiries@periplus.com.sg
Web site: www.periplus.com

**Japan**
Tuttle Publishing
Yaekari Building, 3rd Floor
5-4-12 Ōsaki, Shinagawa-ku, Tokyo
Japan 141-0032
Tel: (03) 5437-0171
Fax: (03) 5437-0755
Email: tuttle-sales@gol.com

**Indonesia**
PT Java Books Indonesia
JI. Kelapa Gading Kirana
Blok A14 No. 17
Jakarta 14240 Indonesia
Tel: (62-21) 451-5351
Fax: (62-21) 453-4987
Email: cs@javabooks.co.id

08 07 06 05    12 11 10 9 8

Printed in the United States of America

TUTTLE PUBLISHING ® is a registered trademark of Tuttle Publishing.

# CONTENTS

# INTRODUCTION

# THE CONSUMMATE SECRET AGENTS

By Boye De Mente

The activities of spies, espionage agents, assassins, terrorists and counter-terrorist forces are now regular news throughout most of the "civilized" world. These agents of death and destruction often utilize scientific technology that makes some of their feats seem almost supernatural.

Many of the professionals in this nefarious and inhuman business learned some of their methods from studying the strategy, tactics and weapons of Japan's infamous feudal-age ninja who practiced the arts of ninjutsu, and were probably the best-trained, most ingenious and deadliest undercover agents of all times.

The roots of ninjutsu have been traced to the Chinese military classic Sun Tzu, written by the famed strategist Sun Wu who lived around 400 B.C. The work was introduced into Japan in the 6th century A.D., where it was carefully studied by the Imperial Court and various clan leaders vieing for power.

Buddhism was introduced in Japan at about the same time, resulting in a conflict between those who wanted to make

Buddhism the state religion and the defenders of Shintoism, the native religion.

The predecessors of Japan's ninja were so-called rebels favoring the adoption of Buddhism who fled into the mountains near Kyoto as early as the 7th century A.D. to escape religious persecution and death at the hands of Imperial forces.

These rebel groups came to be known as yamabushi or "mountain ascetics," who sought enlightenment through pragmatic mysticism. To protect themselves, they combined the study and practice of martial arts and military strategy with psychological warfare and occult powers.

A noted Yamabushi leader began trying to implement a compromise between the backers of Buddhism and the Shintoists, resulting in the Imperial Court sending warriors to invade the mountain domains of the rebels. The attempt to wipe them out failed.

The threat from the Imperial Court continued, however, and over the centuries the yamabushi developed extraordinary survival and fighting skills that made them formidable enemies. By the beginning of Japan's feudal age in 1192, a number of family-clans descended from these rebels had become professional guerrillas and secret agents for hire, and were often retained by the various provincial lords (daimyo) in their inter-clan struggles for supremacy.

Between 1192 and 1333 A.D., a total of 25 ninja "schools" developed, each with its own distinctive techniques and specialties. Ninja training camps flourished throughout the country. During most of this period two of Japan's provinces (now called prefectures) were dominated by ninja clans.

There were more than 50 families in the Koga "school" of ninja in Koga province (now Shiga Prefecture), but only three ninja families, the Hattori, the Momochi and the Fujibayashi, controlled Iga province (now Mie Prefecture). These three were the most famous of feudal Japan's ninja families, the largest of which had over 1,000 members.

## THE GREATEST NINJA BATTLE

The largest recorded gathering of ninja took place on November 3, 1581 when Oda Nobunaga, the most powerful clan leader of the time, led an army of 40,000 warriors against approximately 4,000 Iga ninja in the mountains of Iga province. Only a few of the Iga ninja escaped with their lives.

A short time later, Oda was assassinated by one of his own aides. Oda`s leading general, Ieyasu Tokugawa, immediately began moving to consolidate power in his own hands. He retained the famous ninja leader Hattori and his men to escort him back to his headquarters Okazaki. Later Ieyasu employed the Hattori ninja as his personal body guard, giving them the cover of gardeners on the castle grounds.

In a further move to protect himself and the Shogunate he founded, Ieyasu employed large numbers of the Koga ninja clan in his own secret service. Shortly after this he also brought ninja from other family-clans into the new Shogunate security forces.

As part of his far-reaching plan to solidify and perpetuate the Tokugawa Shogunate, Ieyasu then banned all ninja training camps except those that were to serve the Shogunate, and even prohibitted the mention of the deadly secret agents in any public reference.

In 1637, Ieyasu's grandson and successor, Iemitsu, used several hundred ninja from the Iga clan to help the Shogunate army capture and slaughter some 40,000 Japanese Christians who had taken refuge in a castle in Shimbara. This was to be the last major military action in which ninja played a vital role.

The ninja-turned-Shogunate-security agents and their descendants continued to dominate the police force in Edo (Tokyo) and other Japanese cities down to the 19th century, using their techniques and tactics to identify and capture criminals and enemies of the Tokugawa Shogunate.

Without the intrigue and military competition that existed between Japan's some 270 clan lords daimyo) and the Shogun before the establishment of the Tokugawa period, the fortunes of the "outside" ninja families declined rapidly.

Ninja who were not able to make the transition from secret agents to policeman or government security agents sometimes became outlaws and master criminals. The famous robber Goemon Ishikawa, often referred to as the "Robin Hood" of Japan, had been a ninja lieutenant in the Momochi clan. He was finally captured by Shogunate agents and executed by being boiled alive in a huge cauldron.

Following the downfall of the Tokugawa Shogunate in 1868, the government- sponsored ninja schools were closed down, but several ninja masters continued to practice and teach privately over the next several decades. By the mid- 1900s there were only a few descendants of these families who remembered the old skills, and attempted to carry on some of their traditions as peaceful martial arts. The history and traditions of the ninja are commemorated in a Ninja Museum in Iga-Ueno in present-day Mie Prefecture.

## THE REBIRTH OF THE NINJA

Soon after the end of World War II, Japanese movie-makers began to tap the rich body of historical fact and fiction relating to the ninja, creating a new awareness and appreciation among the current generation of Japanese for the skills and feats of these feudal secret agents.

Hundreds of thousands of Westerners who spent time in Japan were also spell-bound by the movie and TV versions of the remarkable ninja, with their semi-magical powers and derring-do that would put even the most capable Western agent, including James Bond, to shame.

This interest eventually spread to the American movie and television industries, and ninja films became very popular as entertainment around the world. There were some, however, whose interest in the deadly arts of the ninja was for a far more serious purpose.

The author of this book, my colleague and good friend, the late Donn Draeger, was an internationally known authority on Asian martial arts, the author of many books on the subject and a reknowned martial arts teacher.

In this book, Draeger describes not only the feudal environment in which the Japanese ninja flourished, their weapons, techniques, ruses, disguises and various other skills, he also recounts many of their most famous exploits, allowing the reader to vicariously enter the world of the ninja themselves-- as well as that of their victims!

The book not only teaches one a great deal about the psychology and dedication of present-day Japanese, it also gives one valuable insights into the attitudes and behavior of the world's current terrorists, assassins, saboteurs and secret agents.

For those who are not interested in the political and military applications of ninjutsu, the book is filled with the type of intrigue and adventure that makes it read like bestselling fiction.

PHOTO ORION PRESS

## OSAKA CASTLE AT NIGHT

*Formidable and magnificent, its outer walls measured eight miles in circumference. The core of such a fortress was surrounded by a maze of concentric walls which were under constant surveillance. Well-armed sentries were posted on the walls, alert and tuned to all possibilities of danger. The hours of darkness were most dangerous and all warriors became especially watchful for the dreaded Ninja.*

# BECOMING A NINJA

Take a giant mental step back into history. Imagine yourself to be a feudal-age Japanese warrior (bushi), serving a daimyo (clan lord) in the 16th century, a time when all of Japan was in the throes of domestic warfare. Influential clan lords vie with one another in constant attempts to secure positions of military supremacy.

As a fully trained, professional fighting man who specializes in methods of hand-to-hand combat, you have had occasion to take to the field of battle many times in the service of your lord. Each time you resolutely faced death with a state of mental calmness not only expected of a man of your honorable profession but required by the Samurai warrior's sacred ethical code.

Numerous enemy warriors had found your razor-sharp sword always ready, your swordsmanship terrifyingly efficient. Never had you experienced uncertainty as to the outcome of such combat. Always your fighting spirit had seen you through these moments of blood and iron, and the fame of your martial exploits had already made you a well-known hero and legend in your time.

You are well-known as a warrior who fears no man, and the reality of your being alive after more than a decade of fighting attests to the fact that you have never been defeated.

Tonight you are assigned guard duty at your lord's castle. Now, as you stand watch you are fully confident that you will be master of any emergency that might arise. It is your first duty to acquit yourself in such a way as to ensure the safety of your lord. You must also bring credit to him, for the warrior's code requires such loyalty and devotion to him. You are fully prepared to die if necessary to preserve his honor.

But somehow, tonight, your emotional mood is different. As you stand in the chilly blackness of the early spring night, atop the castle's outer rampart, you feel a certain brittle tenseness and a strange and undescribable uneasiness welling up within you.

This feeling is completely new to you. You are puzzled. Your eyes strain to see into the night . . . there is only blackness . . . for the thin slice of the crescent-shaped moon gives little comfort by way of light for your lonely patrol.

Your ears are tuned to catch the slightest sound of danger . . . but you hear none . . . only natural sounds in the spring night. A gentle breeze riffles the surface of the murky waters which fill the moat below you. Reflected on the water's broken surface-pattern is the dim light of the moon.

As you peer over the edge of the rampart, the huge stone wall seems to disappear beneath your feet into blackness some sixty feet to the water below. You know that wall very well . . . it is said to be unclimbable . . . so surely no threat can come from below.

You continue to stare down at the moat, trying to pierce the gloom, for the feeling of tension and uneasiness seems to be produced by your awareness of something . . . or somebody . . . lurking down there.

Your warrior-trained nerves are as tight as a drawn bow-string, and you try desperately to catch the slightest suggestion of unusual movement or sound. There is nothing to be seen or heard, yet the feeling of very tense uneasiness continues, and begins to grow.

You walk along the rampart to a new position, hoping to lose the strange emotion which accompanies you in the lonely night. Then suddenly it tells you the most shameful thing a warrior can learn about himself. You are afraid! Your tenseness, your uneasiness, they are but manifestations of fear . . . pure and simple fear. For the first time in your life you are afraid!

Your mind flashes back to the many times in the past when you faced an enemy. Why were those times so different from now? Facing an enemy who can be seen, his next action anticipated, and your trained reflexes triggered into an appropriate response by his slightest suki (opening), is one thing. But here tonight there is no visible enemy, and that is an entirely different matter.

Now it is suddenly clear to you . . . the reason for your fear . . . your shameful fear. Tonight the fierce commandant of the guard, whom it is said will someday be replaced by you, a brave and loyal warrior, had warned all sentries about the increased activities of the dreaded masters of the art of invisibility . . . the ninja, as these spies and assassins were called . . . who were operating in the hire of your lord's most hated enemy.

All sentries had been cautioned to be especially watchful so that these infiltrators could not bring their unseen and unheard methods of death down upon anyone in the castle.

To the very best of your memory you cannot recall ever having seen a ninja--very few people ever had . . . but you know that they exist. Just last winter you participated in special training exercises designed to cope with these insidious killers who had made their martial art of shinobi or ninjutsu, as it was more popularly called, the most dreaded skill a man could possess.

Ninjutsu encompassed a variety of specialized fighting and espionage skills which made the ninja one of the world's deadliest agents of death and destruction. Indeed, you recall hearing of the clever and terrifying exploits of famous ninja every since you were a young boy.

How well you remember the look of terror on the faces of those persons relating the stories. They told of having seen ninja walk across the surface of water, of them remaining under water for a full day without surfacing, and of how they could walk and run with such stealth that they could approach people without being detected.

Ninja were also reported to have scaled walls that defied ordinary human endeavor. And they could run faster and farther, as well as leap higher, than any normal human being could. It was said that a ninja could even disappear before the very eyes of a pursuer, should he choose to do so. All of these things and many more, even more sensational, were said to be within the capabilities of a ninja.

The townsfolk always made the ninja out as supernatural beings. To a warrior, however, they were flesh and blood, and you never really believed all that you had heard about them . . . or if you did, you felt sure that your sword would show the ninja to be less supernatural than told.

Fear? What was fear but a foolish state of ignorance about something, and the blind acceptance of ignorance was a replacement for reason. But why had this feeling of fear suddenly enveloped you this night? Was it really your ignorance about the ninja that fed the fear?

Here in the darkness of the night, your tour of duty only beginning, you would have ample time to go over what you knew about the ninja and find some explanation to prove to yourself that they were no more than human beings.

Yes! That was the way to rid yourself of this shameful fear which now embarrassed you. Already your confidence is returning . . .

# CHAPTER 1

# HISTORY AND ORGANIZATION

Some of the basic ideas behind the development of ninjutsu came to Japan from China, but like much else in Japanese culture which stems from foreign sources of influence, ninjutsu quickly became Japanized. In Chinese military classics such as the Sonshi (Sun-tzu in Chinese) can be found descriptions of methods of espionage. The Sun-tzu was known in Japan as early as the sixth century A.D.

In the seventh century a considerable number of persons wanted for various reasons by the Imperial Court had taken refuge in the mountainous wilds near Kyoto. They were greatly outnumbered by the government warriors sent out to disperse them, and therefore it became necessary for them to develop clever tactics and strategy to guarantee their survival.

The yamabushi (mountain ascetics) were one such group that had invoked the wrath of the aristocratic court by founding a religion the court believed to be contrary to its best interests.

Prince Regent Shotoku, serving his country in the early years of the seventh century, proved to be a wise and benevolent ruler. But he is generally regarded as the first Japanese ruler to use spies. He used them to determine the facts in civil cases and to improve his means for judgment in deciding these cases. He also used them to investigate and gather intelligence about a particular enemy or potential enemies, to harass them, and to dilute their military prowess.

By the time of the rise to power of the professional Samurai warrior class and the Shogunate form of government in the 12th century, all successful military commanders employed specialists in ninjutsu. They had also made the Sonshi (the Chinese military classic) their standard text.

## THE NINJA FAMILIES

Ninja were born and trained in families devoted to the study and practice of ninjutsu as their profession. Each ninja family was dedicated to a specific tradition (ryu) which characterized its particular brand of espionage and assassination methods. Some seventy different ninjutsu traditions were developed, the most famous of which were those of Iga and Koga provinces on the main island of Honshu.

The ninja clans were found scattered throughout the country, however, their distribution in part due to the fractionization of the older and more organized traditions.

Because individual ninja became attached to and supported different political causes it was possible for father to operate against son, and brother against brother, each in the hire of some very influential land baron who required the services of military spies. But no one ninjutsu organization ever became powerful enough to withstand the onslaught of the combined forces of the Shogun's government.

*Ninja masters were believed to be able to fly on eagles, as depicted here. Ninja did use giant kites to fly over enemy positions*

Secrecy was the foundation upon which all successful ninja depended. Rigid security measures began at the very root of all ninja organizations, that is, within the head family in charge of each particular tradition of ninjutsu. Ninja, when not actually dispatched on missions, resided at base training camps, the locations of which were secret to all but those who belonged to the tradition. A ninja base training camp was always located in a remote mountainous area, in some of the most inaccessible places imaginable.

In order that secrecy surrounding their tradition could be maintained, each tradition established three classes of ninja. At the top level stood the jonin, a high-ranked administrator or boss. He was assisted by the chunin, a small group of middle-ranking ninja whose duties included that of being go- betweens or connecting links between the jonin and the lowest level of ninja, the genin.

It was the genin and his exploits which made the ninja most famous, for they were the men who operated in the field. Though under the strict control of a jonin, it is doubtful whether any genin ever discovered who his boss was. Orders were passed to him through the chunin.

The system was made further complicated by some very clever jonin acting as head of more than one tradition of ninjutsu. In the Koga area alone, over fifty chunin families, each comprised of from 30 to 40 genin, directed all activities of the Koga genin. In Iga, three jonin families controlled all ninja operating under that tradition.

## THE NINJA AND THE LORDS

A daimyo war lord wishing to hire ninja in the furtherance of his military or political cause usually chose and trained his own men, but on occasion he would make contact with ninja leaders through the chunin simply by sending an envoy into the areas where chunin were known to operate. The chunin would find the envoy. The uncertainty of this process of communication was lessened by the constant activities of chunin who were always alert to the possibilities of engaging in espionage.

But the process was fraught with danger to the lord hiring the ninja, for such a contract might result in employing such men who were unfriendly. For this important reason all lords had means of their own by which ninja were to be tested and proven loyal. A newly hired ninja might be given some false data or a meaningless task, the treacherous discloser of which would produce a certain calculated result, sure evidence that the ninja had betrayed his employer.

Then too, ninja who had served a lord faithfully for a period of time could be expected to be approached by enemy ninja who would urge severance of that loyalty.

Lords thus became highly suspicious of ninja in their own hire. Jonin, too, wishing to please their lord clients would dispatch a ninja whom they specially trusted to watch the one operating for a lord; even a third ninja, to watch both might be assigned to a mission.

Because of all the complicated subterfuge connected with the hiring and use of ninja, genin ninja became especially sensitive, always suspicious of all persons, jonin, chunin, and lord alike, and became extremely watchful of all personal contacts, even within their own group.

Ordinary townsfolk considered the ninja as social outcasts, and Samurai warriors looked down upon them as traitorous cowards. Since they were regarded as a pariah class and considered as something less than human, ninja who were captured by warriors usually suffered a horrible death. They might be boiled alive in oil, or have their skin slowly peeled from their bodies.

One particular method of killing a captured ninja was designed to produce a lingering pain and slow death. It consisted of suspending him, having been tightly bound on a wooden frame, over a sharpened bamboo stake. The victim was positioned as though seated in the air with his legs straight and widely stretched; the frame kept the victim from changing his position. The entire load, ninja and frame, was made to hang directly over the stake. When the rope holding the load became wet it elongated and the ninja would slowly be inched downward, anus first, onto the sharp point.

At first a clever ninja might somehow oscillate himself so as to avoid the stake, but as hunger and fatigue set in, his struggles would prove useless. Morning fogs, rains, and heavy dews served to wet the rope sufficiently, but if such natural phenomena did not occur, the ninja's captors would apply water.

Such barbarous treatment helped to make it a common practice for ninja to kill themselves when capture was imminent by taking virulent poisons or stabbing themselves with their own swords. The ninja also disfigured their faces so that they might not be recognized and the source of their ninjutsu traced. A ninja who had been bound would take his own life by simply biting off his tongue, thus producing a fatal hemorrhage.

## NINJA OPERATIONS

Ninja could be dispatched to operate in one or more combinations of five ways: (1) native, (2) inside, (3) living, (4) doubled, and (5) expendable.

The "native" agent was a person of the enemy's regional area who had full knowledge of the customs and geography of that area. Such a ninja was most difficult to sustain inasmuch as his features were well known by the local folk and the enemy warriors. Inside agents were ninja recruited from among the enemy's own officials and personnel. These traitors were chosen from among those who had been deprived of wealth or title, or those who were overly desirous of gaining immediate wealth.

"Living" agents were ninja expected to penetrate the enemy's area, complete their missions, and return to the lord employing them. These men were the most highly trained and clever of ninja. They usually had access to the enemy's area and were not known to be ninja.

The "doubled" agent was an enemy ninja whose loyalty had been switched, by bribes, to a new lord. While they continued in the service of their original lord, they were traitors to his cause. "Expendable" agents were sent, usually unknown to themselves, with false information on their person and into missions which ensured their capture by the enemy.

Not all ninja were known for changeable loyalties. Many were devoted to one war lord and served him with distinction. These ninja were indeed men of courage and though they did not enjoy the social status of the privileged aristocratic warrior, in many respects they equaled the latter in bravery, loyalty, and fighting skill.

## CHAPTER 2

# TRAINING AND SKILLS

A child, either male or female, born into a professional ninja family was expected to carry on the family tradition. Training began at the age of five or six years and was carried out for the remainder of the person's natural life. Five kinds of exercises characterized this training: those of balance, agility, strength, stamina, and various special skills.

One of the first exercises given to youthful trainees was designed to develop a keen sense of balance. A small tree was felled and its branches cut off. The remaining log was placed horizontally about two or three feet off of the ground. Trainees were made to "walk the beam", to turn around on it, to lower themselves, to sit, to rise, even to jump and turn around on it, all without losing balance and falling to the ground.

As skill in keeping his balance grew, the trainee was made to repeat the exercises at greater heights until no fear of high places was felt and he or she was capable of performing incredible feats of balance. One day such a skill would serve the ninja well as he inched his way along narrow areas high on walls, roofs, or in trees.

*Balance training in youthhood*

Training for agility began by making young hopefuls leap over a kind of rope which was suspended between two uprights in full view of the trainee. The nature of the material from which the rope was constructed made this exercise a bit more difficult and dangerous than simply high jumping over a slack rope. A kind of hemp vine which was covered with pirckly thorns was used as the rope. Should the rope be touched in flight over it, its thorns would cause severe lacerations and profuse bleeding.

At an advanced level of skill with this exercise, trainees would in the course of other exercises suddenly come upon this rope which had been stretched in dark or hidden places. Mastery of this exercise laid the basis for the ninja's skill in clearing obstacles which could not be avoided except by jumping over them.

One of the most classic training exercises used for the development of stamina was one which also produced the ability to run swiftly. Ninja had to be superior runners, not only to elude pursuers, but to carry important intelligence, which they had gathered, back to their superiors. All young trainees became familiar with both speed and distance running before they reached their teens.

A special type of straw hat was used to indicate the proper speed of running, simply by placing the hat on the chest as the runner sprinted along. If the runner's speed remained sufficient, the hat would remain stuck to the runner's chest by the force of the wind. A trainee who could maintain this level of speed for long distances developed great stamina. It is reported that ninja were capable of running as much as 50 miles without stopping. Longer distances were usually covered by a series of runners who worked in relays. To some extent stamina determined the ability of ninja to run and walk silently. Terrain conditions also affected this, for it takes different techniques to move silently on surfaces such as loose sand, leaves, wet grass, and hard-packed dirt areas. But breath control entered all methods of running and walking and a ninja learned to hold his body in a peculiar "shoulder shrugged high position" which allowed the optimum intake of air and lessened fatigue and heavy panting.

If a ninja combined walking and running techniques it was possible for him to cover in excess of 100 miles per day, a great tribute to his stamina.

All ninja were aware of the necessity of developing maximum body strength. Training for strength began early and one basic method required a trainee to hang suspended from an overhanging bough using only a double-hand grasp to do so. The older the trainee, the higher he would hang, some 30 to 50 feet being common. A fully trained ninja was expected to hang in this fashion, motionless, for about one hour.

*Endurance training in youthhood*

To every intent and purpose the exercise was also a mental one by which a strong will, resistant to pain, could be developed, though physical benefits centered on the strengthening of fingers, wrists, arms, and shoulders. This ability later gave the ninja confidence in his ability to hang motionless among dense foliage even while his enemies camped directly below him.

## SPECIAL SKILLS OF THE NINJA

It was the category of special skills which marked the ninja out as a near super-human person. No training or technique that might prove useful to him in his profession was overlooked.

In his youth the ninja made special preparations to develop a unique body. Then, when bones were soft and ligatures and tendons pliable, he learned to stretch and manipulate his joints so that he might dislocate them, under control, from their normal positions. This strange skill came into good use in the event he was captured. If bound up by his captors he could effect his own release by appropriate dislocations and stretching actions. A ninja who was being trussed up always expanded his body as much as possible, for later by simply relaxing, he greatly loosened his bonds.

If it became necessary for the ninja to squeeze through small openings, he could do so by manipulation of his joints. The skill was also useful in certain aspects of hand-to-hand combat such as at the time an enemy applied a painful jointlock against the ninja. By dislocation techniques the ninja could minimize the pain and actually escape from the leverage being applied.

The ninja's expertise at walking was the result of the use of ten styles or techniques:

31

1. Nuki ashi.......Stealthy step
2. Suri ashi.......Rub step
3. Shime ashi......Tight step
4. Tobi ashi.......Flying step
5. Kata ashi.......One step
6. So ashi.........Big step
7. Ko ashi.........Little step
8. Kakizami........Small step
9. Wari ashi.......Proper step
10. Tsune ashi......Normal step

But he also used another interesting method called yoko-aruki or "side walking." By a specific technique of moving the legs sideways in cross-step fashion, the ninja confused the enemy. Tracks left by this method do not reveal which direction the ninja is traveling. Side walking also had uses in narrow passages or lanes such as found in castle corridors or in bamboo groves.

Swimming was one of the ninja's most reliable skills. He was trained to move through water for great distances, silently, but not in a particularly swift manner. By use of his special swimming techniques the ninja could negotiate a moat without being seen or heard. He could, if called upon to do so, swim with great loads, using self-made flotation devices. The use of powerful and very skillful strokes made the ninja able to swim against tides and currents or to cut across them. If caught in water plants and sea-weed, he used still other stroking methods to disentangle himself.

A special vertical kind of swimming enabled him to carry things to their destination without wetting them. He could actually write while swimming and keep the paper from becoming water-soaked. The ninja also practiced hand-to-hand combat in and under water, learning to fight with and without weapons. He was equally skilled at grappling with an enemy on the deck of a boat, and could cleverly manage to hurl both himself and his enemy, locked in combat, into water where his skill would greatly reduce the chances for survival of the enemy. By other methods of swimming the ninja could keep himself afloat and in position to fire arrows or firearms, his powerful legs making this possible.

*Under water training*

Breath control methods gave him the ability to remain under water for about three minutes. Longer periods were made possible by use of special breathing devices. Diving and swimming under water involved precision techniques useful in avoiding detection or the missiles fired by his enemies. The ninja knew precisely at which depth he must swim in order to avoid arrows, spears, or rifle balls.

The ninja's ability to suppress his breathing was useful in more ways than in running, walking, and swimming. Breath control often became important as a life-saving technique when the ninja went into hiding near a position occupied by an enemy. The slightest sound made by either inhalation or exhalation would surely bring a spear or sword thrust his way.

Some ninja reduced their breathing by methods of concentration. Others relied upon mechanical means such as placing a small piece of cotton flannel cloth in the mouth to muffle the flow of air.

## NINJA DISGUISES

It was necessary for the ninja to train himself to recognize a wide variety of sounds without sighting the person or object causing them. The noises usually made by gates or doors as they were being opened and closed not only told the ninja what specific dimensions were involved, but in which direction these portals lay. The ninja was also able to quickly judge the number of persons in a room from the sounds of their breathing, their steps, and the rustling of their garments.

A tell-tale rhythmic breathing also enabled him to distinguish a light from a heavy sleeper, a false sleep from a genuine one, knowing that a person feigning sleep is tense enough for his body to emit sounds as the joints moved ever so slightly, if under muscular strain.

The ninja was an exceptionally good dancer. He was trained to dance folk rhythms so that he could, under appropriate conditions, mingle with the people of a specific region and thereby learn more about the target to which he had been assigned. Since the ninja had to conceal his true identity, he had to make use of disguises, with which he physically transformed himself and imitated somebody useful to the accomplishment of his mission.

Disguises included those of: (1) warriors, (2) farmers, (3) artisans, (4) theatrical artists, (5) merchants, and (6) monks, priests, or nuns. But clever disguise was often not enough, for the ninja had also to be able to copy the social and personal mannerisms of the person being imitated. The best physical transformation would be compromised if the ninja failed in the other aspects of his deceptive ruse.

Considerable study of different social classes of people had to be made by ninja in order to effect thir disguises, and so skillful did some of them become that they retained their false identities for years without being discovered. For example, if a ninja wished to operate in the disguise of a priest, it was necessary for him to become competent in performing the religious duties of the clergy.

As a master of deception the ninja was also competent in the use of camouflage to conceal his whereabouts. Both natural and man-made objects served to let him carry out his insidious activities without being seen. For example, the ninja arranged to disappear from sight by jumping into a hole in the ground which had been filled with the fine ashes of the paulownia tree (shinobi bai). From a distance the hole was invisible. Because of such deceptions many persons credited the ninja with supernatural powers.

## NINJA IN THE FIELD

Intelligence work such as the ninja was constantly engaged in required that he have a functional knowledge of map-making and reading. The ability to accurately sketch the enemy's positions and deployments or to commit a diagramatic estimate of other important matters to paper was indispensable to all ninja.

Every ninja worked hard to train himself as a competent woodsman. He lived off the land. Additionally, he depended on caches specially made for his needs, and at other times from what he was able to pilfer from local inhabitants.

A kind of pickled plum not only gave him some food value, but contained salt which increased his resistance to physical breakdown under vigorous and protracted exercise. Specially compounded tablets were the ninja's food rations--light in weight, space presrving, and carried on his person. They were to be used at times when normal food was unavailable. The actual ingredients for these tablets were considered secret, but most of them contained buckwheat flour, wheat germ, potato flour, Job's tears, carrots, and a kind of grass, chopped finely and compressed into tablet form.

Anti-thirst pills, made from plum syrup and other ingredients, kept the ninja from depending on native water supply points which were sometimes not only polluted but also poisoned in the hope of catching a ninja off guard. Ninja rarely used water from sources near people, always distrusting it. Ninja could recognize water that had been poisoned by the peculiar way it reflected their persons.

Wandering in wild areas the ninja was warned of the location of settlements by dung and other signs from domestic animals. Always cautious, he might deliberately flush a flock of wild birds, knowing that birds in flush-flight never travel in the direction of a settlement. Chirping birds and insects told him that there was no human life in the area; but when those natural noises stopped, he became alert.

Rutted roads made by people who tend to follow the same

path told of proximity to settlements. Paths made by animals became less depressed and ridged than those made by humans. Should snow cover the ground the ninja determined the whereabouts of roadways by thrusting a stick into the snow and feeling the contour of the ground.

High in the mountains, a ninja was most cautious about his movements between the hours of ten in the morning and four in the afternoon. During these hours the snow is usually soft and may slip, causing dangerous snow slides. If a ninja lost his way, he would fell a large tree and read the pattern of its annual rings; the widest ring always faces south.

Living a rugged life as an outcast from society he learned to acclimatize his body to the weather of all seasons. He learned that rice straw woven into a long garment would act as a water-repellent coat against rain, and that bark beaten into cloth served as the basis for garments which insulated him from cold. Certain hides and furs also provided the materials for his clothing.

# CHAPTER 3

# OPERATING TECHNIQUES

The best hours of operation for the ninja who wished to remain unseen were naturally those of darkness, which permitted him to blend with natural or other backgrounds. For extremely critical night missions, the ninja prepared his vision by keeping himself in the dark at least 24 hours prior to the mission. He spent the daylight hours deep in a dark cave or in a small hole he had fashioned in the earth where he could cover and conceal himself until it was time to depart on his mission.

The sensitivity of a ninja's eyes at night thus verged on the fantastic. He was able to read signs and other written material even on the darkest night. To aid the development of such visual power, the ninja kept to a steady diet of vitamin A rich foods such as watercress, which grew wild in the countryside streams.

In his approach to a structure he planned to enter, the ninja was often bothered by barking dogs. He made short work of them with specially prepared scraps of poisoned fish he carried in a small pouch. It was extremely easy to introduce poison into fish and the meat held up well on impact with the ground. The ninja might have to toss a piece of fish many tens of yards to get it in front of the beast he wished to kill.

*The Ninja in full costume*

Once on the grounds of the building he was to enter the ninja chose his method of entrance with extreme care. Hinged doors usually emitted squeaking noises from their rusty hinges. This could be eliminated by applying oil, water, or, at times when the former two materials were unavailable, urine. Sliding doors too could emit tell-tale noises, so the ninja carefully dampened the grooves in which they slid before moving them.

## DANGERS WITHIN WALLS

Feudal buildings in Japan had characteristics which made it relatively easy for a ninja to break into them. He particularly liked the false attic air spaces above their ceilings. Entrance from small openings outside the roof was possible if the ninja used his skill in dislocating his body to make himself small enough to inch his way through such openings. Once inside the false attic, the ninja quickly found the inner trapdoors which led to the inside of the building proper.

The darkness of rooms inside a building was ideal for the operations of ninja, for only candlelight or light from oil lamps illuminated the areas where persons gathered. The ninja, wearing his special black costume, was invisible under these conditions.

But danger lay at every turn in the building. Hallway floor plankings were specially sprung to emit creaking noises when trod upon. To avoid being detected, the ninja devloped a special technique of walking, or he could work his way spider-like across the ceilings. Specially prepared false flooring, triggered by body weight, often greeted the prowling ninja and hurled him into a deep pit onto sharpened bamboo stakes. Or such a pit would simply contain him until house guards could

41

arrive and kill him with their spears.

Ninja were acrobatic and used this ability to walk on their hands when conditions warranted this procedure. This was done to avoid objects which might be set low to the ground. Occasionaly the ninja simply crawled on all- fours to avoid similar obstacles.

Among the warning devices most dreaded by ninja were those composed of hair-like threads which criss-crossed an area in which a ninja was most likely to pass. The threads, which were connected to objects that rattled or clanged, would be activated upon contact with the ninja's body and were devilishly hard to locate. Some of these threads could be rendered useless by cutting, but others would operate when severed; thus the ninja developed a special skill in selective slow-stepping, placing his feet down between the threads, being most careful not to touch them.

He knew guards could lurk quietly in a dark room, almost unnoticed until the ninja came into range of spear or sword thrust. One method by which the ninja avoided such a threat was to move slowly with his sword and scabbard held out in front of him in such a way that he had a margin of safety between a potential adversary and himself. On contact with an inanimate object, the scabbard would make a sound which told the ninja there was no immediate danger.

But if the scabbard touched a guard, the guard would most likely go into action believing the scabbard to be the ninja himself; at which the ninja could dislodge the scabbard and have his sword ready for instant counteraction.

Before a ninja went about his work in a room he made sure that all the occupants were sleeping. Aside from the methods of recognizing a true sleeping state from a false one by charactristics of breathing, the ninja could utilize another simple test: sprinkling finely ground rice dust on the face of a person who appeared to be sleeping. He who feigned sleep would react immediately, perhaps thinking he was being poisoned, and would then be silenced by the ninja's sword. A person sound asleep would not stir.

## TRICKS OF THE TRADE

By his intensive training, and the special skills he developed as a result of it, the ninja could be counted on to do things that seemed impossible to ordinary men. Take the example of ninja who had been trapped in buildings which had been set afire to drive them out into the open. Many of them disappointed their would-be captors by remaining inside, thereby supposedly suffering a horrible death.

But the ninja were always prepared for fire. Knowing that the deadly accumulation of gases could suffocate a man, they feared smoke more than the flames. But less than a scant inch from the floor there is always enough air to sustain life and the ninja made good use of this shallow air zone. He could also be counted on to break his way through the flooring and to dig a small hole into which he would work his body and escape from the heat and flames by covering himself with soft earth until the blaze -- and his would-be captors -- had vanished. Then, unharmed, he would emerge to continue his mission.

If assassination was the purpose of his assigned mission, the ninja usually struck at his victims when they least expected an attack. Usually moments of triumph, of celebration, or of leisure afforded the best times for him to make his attempt at assassination. A lord ordered killed was most easily taken after he had spent a good portion of his evening in drunken carousal.

At other times, a lord enjoying his pursuit of sexual

pleasures might be an even easier victim. One favorite method of effecting the dispatch of such a victim was for a ninja to hide himself under the floor of the room in which the lord was disporting himself. Previously obtained information on the favorite seat and the reclining habits of the potential victim made it easy for the ninja to jab a short spear through the flimsy floor boards, matting, and bedding, with often fatal results. Even working in such cramped quarters was an easy matter for the ninja, trained as he was to perform his special skills from all conceivable positions and angles.

Should a ninja be captured before he could escape or at least take his own life, he knew that cruel and inhuman treatment lay in store for him. But he most likely would undergo severe questioning before being killed, in the hope of getting him to reveal his base location, his operational secrets, and the person behind his mission. In the struggle which preceded full capture of the ninja, the captors quickly discovered how difficult it was to subdue him. By special training he knew how to make his body feel heavier and more awkward if he was to be lifted or thrown. Special positions made this possible.

Then too, the ninja was a master technician in the use of a wide range of vicious weapons. To take him alive was no easy task. His acrobatic fighting skill was a source of constant amazement and difficulty to even the finest warrior.

A ninja's intensive training made him aware of the benefit of utilizing natural phenomena to aid him in concealing his movements. The light of the moon could be a disadvantage, so he would usually wait for the moon to dip into a cloud bank before taking any critical action. On cloudless nights when the moon shone brightly, the ninja usually remained inactive. Wind, rain, and the general confusion of the elements in tempest were a blessing to such a man, for the sounds thus created masked his movements and any noise he might inadvertently make.

The ninja also had considerable knowledge of human psychology and took advantage of the lulling and hypnotic effect which bad weather such as a downpour of rain can have on people. He usually operated in bad weather, even in the worst storms.

# OPERATING SKILLS

Perhaps the most dominant skill of the ninja was his ability with weapons. He was an efficient fighter with all major weapons and a host of minor ones. The sword, spear, halberd, and bow and arrow were his constant companions, but throwing blades, sickles, chains, and strange-looking, little-known weapons were also an important part of his arsenal. He learned in his training days to make gunpowder, bombs, flares, and missiles for firearms. He was able to utilize the urea found in the soil near lavatories as the base for his nitrogen supply in the making of gunpowder. He knew how to nitrate the wood ash from open fires so that it could be made into explosive mixtures.

The ninja was also adept in methods of lassoing and binding an enemy and could tie a victim so securely that self-escape was impossible. Some ways of binding were so severe that if the victim struggled against his bonds in an attempt to free himself he would succeed only in tearing out his testicles or painfully constricting them to the extent of rendering himself unconscious.

The ninja was a communications expert. Fire and smoke signals were utilized on the basis of prearranged codes to transmit messages over long distances, relay fashion, to his base. Flags, gestures, and the arrangement of natural objects to provide codes signals were still other media of communication open to the ninja. He wrote messages with lemon juice, knowing that heat would make the contents of such messages visible. Often such lemon- juice writings were made under visible characters which had no real importance should they be intercepted.

But the ninja was even more clever. He sometimes used a specially prepared and colorless ink made from a bitter compound. The message written with this ink was only readable when traced with the tongue. Under threat of capture, or when messages were no longer useful and could not be destroyed by other means, the ninja would simply swallow the material on which it was written. But a special skill perfected by the ninja allowed him to disgorge a message which he had swallowed, should it become necessary for him to hide a message in this fashion. That technique made is possible for the ninja to drink tea and eat a full meal with the "swallowed" message lodged in his throat and later quietly recover it. Or a message that had been encased in a special kind of wax would be swallowed and then recovered from the ninja's stool.

## POISON AND SEX

The ninja were excellent horsemen. Though persons other than nobles and warriors were forbidden to ride horses, it was sometimes necessary for a ninja to make good his escape on horseback. And he had no peers at riding.

Skills with medicines made him his own doctor, and he could allay and cure the effects of insect bites, poisonous plants, intestinal disorders, and the general ailments from which he occasionaly suffered. Wounds which might otherwise become infected were treated with special molds placed in poltice form directly on the wounded area.

Ninja were even known to have skillfully amputated their own limbs in order to avoid the danger of capture or the possibly fatal effects of an infectious wound.

*Ninja often used deadly blow-guns
with poisoned darts to kill victims.*

Perhaps no ninja was without technical skills in the compounding and usage of terrible poisons. Considerable knowledge of the human anatomy and its physiology made possible the concoction of poisons or debilitating agents to be

47

used against enemies. Each ninjutsu tradition had its own special preparations. Some were subtle poisons. Those which had been derived from the livers and other organs of animals such as toads and bears, spiders and wasps, snakes and lizards, were especially lethal. Mixed in proper porportions and put into tea, rice wine, or foodstuffs, these poisons would do their deadly work quickly and silently.

Some ninja even had the ability to saturate a hand-fan with a poisonous but pleasant-smelling substance. When the fan was used, the user succumbed to the poisonous vapors. Poisons were also used against the ninja, in hope of trapping them. Water and food supplies were frequently prepared and left for ninja to find. As a consequence, all ninja developed antidote thrapy to a high degree.

In his study of human psychology the ninja made extensive investigations of the sexual behavior of his potential enemies. Man in his frequent amorous moments exhibits weaknesses in judgment, alertness, and general decorum like at no other time in his life. War lords in particular, given to extravagances of all kinds, delighted in the amassing of large numbers of concubines.

When any one particular war lord proved to be unapproachable by normal means the ninja assigned to assassinate him might enlist the services of a female ninja, usually a beautiful and talented dancer. It would be arranged for her to eventually be requested to dance at the enemy lord's castle. So great would be her physical beauty that the lord could not resist her charms and would order her to occupy his bed. It was then a simple matter for the woman ninja to introduce an appropriate poison into her female organ which, later during the night's sexual play, would poison the lord and cause his death.

In the case of lords who preferred a chigo, a young boy

page, as a partner for sodomy, the boy, having first been placed under extreme obligation to the ninja, could similarly poison his host.

## UNMASKING A NINJA

A ninja's training experiences developed within him a set of conditioned reflexes which often proved to be his own downfall. All warriors knew this fact and made efforts to make ninja trap themselves. The process of self- entrapment depended on the fact that a conditioned reflex is an automatic response to some imposed stimulus; that such a response cannot be easily checked by the will. When a person suspected of being a ninja, and dangerous to a particular political cause, was carefully watched, he could not prevent himself from revealing the true nature of his skills with ninjutsu.

At some time during the surveillance a carefully laid plan could expose him. One method by which this was accomplished was for the lord to arrange for small children to be playing in the area in which the suspected ninja moved. At least one of the children would be bribed into tossing a spinning top directly into the path of the suspected ninja.

If the suspect was indeed a ninja, he would nimbly avoid the top by a light and skillful dodging or jumping action of which only a trained ninja would be capable. Once this action betrayed the ninja, the lord's men would immediately converge on him and attempt to capture him.

# CHAPTER 4

# COSTUME, TOOLS AND WEAPONS

When operating without disguise the ninja always wore a special costume called shinobi shozoku. It consists of four parts: (1) jacket, (2) trousers, (3) hood or scarf, and (4) shoes.

The most common color of the ninja's costume was that of a reddish-black hue. Its lining was designed to be used in a reversible fashion and was either a deep persimmon or deep blue color. These shades blend well with the blackness of the night and make the ninja most difficult, if not impossible, to see.

The jacket and trousers contained numerous pockets or pouch-like recesses in which the ninja concealed the many assorted objects necessary to his operation. Certain objects were always carried by every ninja, but special objects were chosen in accordance with the nature of the assigned mission.

Thus it was not at all unusual for a ninja to produce from his person, the tools he needed to force entry into some structure,

51

the tools he needed to scale a high wall, a snorkle should he be forced to go under water to elude his pursuers, smoke and incendiary bombs, flares, anti-personnel bombs, a flotation device by which to carry heavy loads across water, a collection of wild field mice, lizards, or weasels to be used to scatter and distract people, emergency food and water supplies, medicines and poisons, as well as a variety of weapons with which to fight.

Lightweight but durable split-toe cloth-canvas shoes provided the ninja with an appropriate foothold for his difficult feats. Two kinds of soles were commonly used: one of a rubber or gum-like substance to give good traction, and another of a special cotton-floss material which made the silent step of the ninja even more quiet. Both kinds of soles were carried by each ninja.

By his use of the hood or scarf the ninja could not only mask his face and head outline to avoid detection but could rely upon their special properties to filter water for drinking purposes, to act as a mask to filter smoke, to act as an antiseptic binding for wounds, or to serve as a weapon with which to defend himself.

What was especially important about the ninja's costume and gear was that all of it was of a lightweight, portable nature, designed to be worn or carried without overburdening him. The fact that a ninja fully garbed and equipped could still move rapidly with agility speaks of the cleverness with which the ninja made his equipment and used it.

But even without his standard costume, such as when he was traveling and operating under a disguise, the ninja was never without a good share of his tools and weapons which he managed to secure in whatever costume he was using. The choice of these tools and weapons depended on the nature of his mission.

## WATER TOOLS

Water-crossing operations presented no real difficulties to the ninja. Portable boats and flotation devices took him safely across bodies of water which were not to be negotiated by swimming. The kama ikada was a small straw raft which folded and could be back-carried under the ninja's costume. The shinobi-bune and the kagata hasami-bune were types of small portable boats, too large to be carried hidden, but which were laid in caches near the point where they would be used.

Ukigusa was another flotation device, which doubled as a lantern. This cylindrical object was made of a flexible fish bone ribbing over which oiled paper was  stretched and glued into place. One end was sealed, the other provided with a small trapdoor. A candle placed inside of the cylinder served to give fair illumination to the nocturnal traveler, but the trapdoor closed and the cylinder inverted when held in water, trapping a pocket of air the volume of the cylinder and giving buoyancy to the ninja. Depending upon the amount of buoyancy needed, the ninja could hold one or more ukigusa between his legs or tie them to his body so that he floated upright in water with his hands free to accomplish other tasks.

Several larger ukigusa could be tied to a heavy object to float it on the surface of water or even just under the surface, to keep it from being spotted by the enemy.

The mizugumo were pontoon instruments used to support the ninja in an erect position atop the water. This gave him the appearance of walking over the surface of the water and many a superstitious townsman reported the supernatural powers of the ninja because of this illusion.

If the ninja had to submerge, his mizu zutsu or bamboo snorkle tube would allow him to remain under water almost as long as he wished. Extremely clever ninja had even devised a snorkle which appeared to be nothing but a smoking pipe. Thus, in disguise, mingling with townsfolk a ninja could, when necessary, enter the water and disappear before the eyes of bewildered watchers who saw no special apparatus to aid this feat.

But a ninja who had been surprised and had fled into water to elude his enemy might not be equipped with any kind of snorkle. In such cases necessity truly became the mother of extemporaneous invention. The ninja would attempt to pick a reed grass or bamboo tube during his flight to the water, or even pluck such reed material as was already growing in the water, to serve as his snorkle.

When these measures failed, he would use his specially prepared scarf to trap a large air bubble as he dove into the water. Such an air bubble provided a limited reservoir for breathing, usually less than 10 minutes, but gave the ninja a chance to make good his escape by some other subterfuge.

Occasionally a ninja provided himself and his mates with secret fords over wide rivers. Stones were laid submerged some distance below the surface of the water, spaced several feet apart. The precise locations of these fords were closely guarded secrets. They might even be relocated periodically to avoid compromise. A casual observer from afar might really believe that a ninja was able to walk over the surface of water should he see one crossing a river by means of the submerged stepping stones.

Narrow bodies of water might also be crossed by means of a trolley device called the kassha. A rope, anchored on one side of the body of water, would be carefully concealed and led under water to the opposite bank. This point of termination was known only to the ninja.

In quick flight the ninja would pick up the loose end of the rope so concealed, securing it to his pulley device which he carried in his costume. By this means he could quickly glide across the water and drop safely on the other side. Even if his pursuers cut the line the ninja could swing free to the other bank or, after dropping into the water, escape by such underwater methods as the snorkle.

## SCALING TOOLS

Scaling operations faced the ninja on almost every mission. Whether confronted with a simple earthen garden wall, the wooden wall of a structure, or a huge stone wall such as surrounded a medieval castle, the ninja was prepared to climb. By use of the ne-kade (cat claw) or te-kagi (hand key) the ninja was able to grip relatively smooth, hard surfaces. These instruments, worn on the hands like gloves, enabled him to stick to wall surfaces and haul himself upward.

He could also depend on his musubinawa, a special length of twisted horse's hair, easy to fold and conceal, and unbelievably durable. It was useful in hauling himself upward and would support triple his body weight. By use of the musubinawa the ninja could also lash himself to inaccessible places. The shinobi kumade was a device made up of short pieces of bamboo which telescoped and shortened into a convenient length and could be hidden inside the ninja's costume. A rope extended the entire length of this device, to one end of which was fastened a grappling hook to provide purchase. The locked sections formed a stiff pole for climbing.

Various other rope ladders and devices were carried and employed on special occasions, all used in combination with the standard tools. Thus to the ninja, there was no such thing as an unclimbable wall. Each construction challenged the ninja who sought to disprove its invulnerability. If climbing some object was outside the intended capabilities of his equipment, the ninja would design such new tools as would make the task possible.

*Horse-hair ropes were often used by ninja
to scale high walls.*

In his initial approach to a compound he planned to enter, the ninja relied upon his tools to effect this important phase of his mission. The application of tools had to be made in the strictest requirement of silence, for an unusual noise would surely alert the sentries on duty. Entry into a castle was perhaps the most dangerous, and most challenging, of all missions; not only because the castle was teeming with watchful sentries, but because it could be counted on to be designed as a confusing concentric compound made up of false approaches and deadend avenues meant to trap unwary infiltrators.

*"Cat's claws" fighting device*

## INFILTRATION

All began at the moat. It had to be negotiated unseen, and silently. The greatest problem arose from the fact that the ninja had to be skilled enough so as not to disturb the natural sounds of the animals which inhabited the water. Wild fowl who swam on the surface or nested on the moat's outer banks could easily be aroused into noisy confusion by a careless movement.

Frogs, normally croaking in concert, would stop their chorus if disturbed. Any such change in the background of sounds would serve to warn sentries. But a ninja skillful in moat crossing operations avoided such complications by poisoning the fowl and spreading a chemical mixture over the surface of the water which caused frogs to croak loudly for a short period of time.

Likewise, the outer wall of the castle rampart which rose from out of the moat was not the main problem which faced the ninja. .He could scale it, unseen and silently, but here again, except during the coldest winter season, he had to contend with the sounds of nature. Crickets living in the stones of the wall, would, if disturbed, stop making their characteristic chirping noise. To offset this undesirable possibility the ninja carried a supply of crickets under the influence of a chemical mixture which caused them to chirp.

The outer perimeter of any compound, but especially that of a castle, would be under heavy guard. It was most essential to the ninja that he avoid contact. Not only were warriors strong and fearless men skilled in fighting with vicious weapons, but any encounter with a sentry might delay the timing of his mission and further create a disturbance which would bring more guards down upon him. Therefore, a ninja preferred to bypass sentries. Recourse to taking a sentry's life was a last measure. Strangulation was the favored method. A ninja could slip quietly behind a sentry and by means of a special weapon, choke the life out of him, without any sound being heard. The lifeless body would then be tied and hung to dangle over the castle wall or hidden out of sight so that it could not alert a sentry who might later pass by.

Rarely did a ninja use a knife or sword to dispatch a sentry. Unless the stroke of the blade was perfect, the sentry might call out. Then too the quantity of blood which would be spilled by this method would serve to warn others that an enemy was operating inside the castle.

Once inside a compound the ninja could expect to be faced with the problem of forcing entry into locked areas. From within the pockets of his costume he produced the necessary assorted tools used such as the fork-shaped tsuba-giri, an instrument used to spring doors and to cut locks; the shikoro, a pointed saw with which to cut through metal or wood; the kunai, a thin spatulate- shaped knife used to dig holes or bore; and the tobi-kunai, a multi-purpose tool which was used to pry, dig, bore, cut, wedge, and perform a variety of useful operations. The ninja picked locks with the osaku or the juroro-kagi but could also chisel out a lock, which resisted all other means, with his tatami nomi.

After making entry the ninja might wish to keep others from making easy entrance into the room in which he intended to operate. To block such passage the ninja installed special locking devices on the doors and panels leading to the area. Though he was trained to operate in the dark the ninja sometimes required a bit of light. Specially made candles fixed and shielded to focus on a spot area provided such minimal illumination and did not draw the attention of those who might pass near where the ninja was working.

## NINJA WEAPONS

Though every ninja was trained as a fighting man, he was largely a defensive fighter. And while he could rarely afford the luxury of a uni- purpose tool or weapon, the fact that many of his tools could be substituted for weapons did not prevent the ninja from designing a wide variety of weapons which were quite dissimilar from those used by the warriors. The weapons of the ninja had to be of the variety that could be easily concealed or those which appeared to the casual eye to be harmless everyday implements.

It would not be practical for the ninja to be a specialist in only one particular kind of weapon. Nor could he afford to have only a vague kind of familiarity with a variety of weapons. The ninja had to be master of as many as he could possibly expect to use. Some were qualified to use as many as 20 different weapons. But the ninja, unlike the aristocratic warrior with his sword, had no central weapon.

The sword, which served the warrior as his "living soul" and around which a mystique had been woven, was carried by the ninja but had no special meaning for him except that of utility. The ninja's sword (ninja-to) was not a particularly valuable or fine one. It lacked the attention to metallurgical and decorative artistry that was characteristic of many of the warriors' blades. For one thing, the ninja's sword was shorter than that of the warrior, which made it necessary for him to assume a fighting posture with the drawn sword in which the arm was fully extended. A warrior rarely would do so.

The scabbard of a ninja's sword (saya) was considerably longer than the blade it housed. This provided a space at the bottom of the scabbard in which something could be concealed. Common use of that space found it filled with a chemical mixture which could be thrown or blown into the faces of pursuers to temporarily blind them. The scabbard also could serve as an underwater snorkle tube, as a club, and sometimes as a lever.

The handguard (tsuba) of the ninja's sword was much larger than that found on the warrior's sword. It served as a foot tread. When the sheathed sword was placed upright against the base of some object, the weapon might function as a small ladder to give the first important step upward in

*A ninja with a deadly chain weapon.*

negotiating a relatively low barrier. Once above the barrier, the ninja could haul his sword up by means of the long cord (sageo) attached to it. Tht same cord could be employed as a tourniquet or the means by which to bind or strangle a victim.

61

# THE FIGHTING STAFF

All ninja were expert at bojutsu (the art of the fighting staff). The staff is a particularly effective weapon in a fight against any hand-to-hand weapon. A single operator armed with the staff and skilled in its use can give a good account against as many as five enemies. A staff could be found in natural form but was usually carved from hardwood and of a length to suit the ninja. Several such staff weapons could be hidden along the ninja's expected route of approach and escape, to provide a reliable weapon for emergency use.

Sometimes a ninja used his staff to vault over barriers. The shinobi zue was a hollow staff. Contained inside of it was a length of weighted chain which could be flung out at the enemy at the proper moment to flail him into submission, to ensnare him or his weapon, or to lasso an overhanging object in order to provide a purchase for climbing. The shinobi zue was most usually carried by ninja disguised as priests, since it was quite common for a man of the clergy to be seen carrying a staff.

One composite weapon which was always a part of the ninja's paraphernalia was the kusarigama. A wooden handle to which a sickle blade was hafted at right angles, and a weighted chain made up the design of this unusually effective instrument. The ninja's kusarigama was of necessity smaller than that of the warrior, for it had to be carried concealed. But its effect, as a tool or weapon, was respected by all warriors who had faced it in combat. The ninja used this weapon to slash and stab at his enemy, parrying or blocking the enemy's weapon, or perhaps ensnaring the enemy or his weapon to render his victim helpless.

The ninja could also flail the enemy with a powerful swing of the weighted chain. By using the chain as a lasso the ninja could obtain purchase to haul himself upward over some barrier or lower himself over a wall.

A strange-looking weapon quite similar to the kusarigama was the kyoketsu shoge. This small hand sickle had an additional blade appendange which projected from the blade proper. A length of animal hair, braided into a strong cord, had a ring-like poise attached to its far end and was secured to the butt end of the hand sickle.

Facing an enemy, the ninja would throw the poise at his intended victim who would most probably catch it. Then the ninja skillfully shot a coiled loop over the victim's hand which held the poise and before the startled enemy realized it, he was bound fast at that point and being hauled in by the ninja who would engage him with his hand sickle. Should the victim cut the cord, the ninja simply threw the sickle or used some other weapon.

The shinobi kai was a short harmless-looking length of bamboo tubing. Hidden inside of it was a length of weighted chain which could be used to flail or ensnare a victim at close quarters.

## THE DEADLY SHURIKEN

One of the most useful of all weapons to the ninja was the shuriken. Since each ninja designed his own particular type, there were countless patterns of these small hand-held throwing blades. Shuriken usually took the shape of short stick-like lengths of iron which had been pointed and possibly flattened somewhat and sharpened; but they could also be star-shaped instruments. The stick-like shuriken could be thrown to tumble in flight or so that they traveled directly to the target. This kind of shuriken was the most difficult to master, but when it struck the target it penetrated deeply.

The star-shaped shuriken tumbled in flight and their many points made it easy for the ninja to stick them into the target; but the depth of penetration they afforded was far less than what could be achieved with the straight bladed ones. A wafer-thin shuriken, with a small hole in its middle, whistled hideously as it sped to the target. The hole allowed the instrument to be used as a nail puller.

*Shuriken and tools*

Maximum effective range of the shuriken was limited to about thirty feet. A ninja usually carried nine of them. He considered this number a lucky one. The most advanced technique for throwing shuriken was that which required the least possible movement. A ninja in a hidden position could thus deliver his weapons without detection. Anybody struck by a shuriken might not suffer a fatal injury but would be rendered combatively ineffective if the blade buried itself into his face, throat, or head. The severe puncture caused by the shuriken made healing a difficult and painful process.

When being pursued, and while on the run, the ninja would very often throw shuriken into the ground behind him. The blade portion which projected upward from the ground offered a hard-to-see source of danger to his pursuers who might step on the blade. But for this defensive purpose the ninja more often employed a special weapon known as the tetsu-bishi, a caltrop, which was made in the shape of a pyramid of twisted sharp-pointed metal spines. Tetsu-bishi were always sprinkled liberally on the ground directly in the paths of pursuing enemies. Sometimes the tetsu-bishi was thrown as a shuriken.

Unexcelled ingenuity provided the ninja with a variety of useful projectile weapons. Poisoned needles, darts, and blinding powders (metsubushi), blown from blowpipes, were useful at close quarters. Some ninja mastered the deadly skill of fukibari-jutsu which involved the blowing of needles from the mouth. A small bow (hankyu) served to shoot short arrows for anti-personnel missions but would also carry fire bombs and incendiary devices into targets for missions of arson.

The nage teppe, or hand grenade, was used to destroy concentrations of enemy warriors. Eggs which had been emptied of their normal contents, served as shells to carry chemicals. A ninja disguised as a merchant was never without such a weapon which exploded with a flash on being broken in the faces of enemies bent on pursuit after the ninja. The sode tsutsu was a crude shotgun which had only a short effective range. But its spray of small pellets was deadly.

The kakae ozutsu, a large-barreled mortar made of wood and reinforced with paper, had a longer range and more deadly effect. Because it was made of wood and paper, it was highly portable and could be moved quickly to be fired in another sector to defend ninja operations. Sometimes fuses were attached to shuriken; they fizzled and sparked vigorously on their way to the target and more often than not panicked the intended victim who probably mistook them for bombs.

By use of the uzume-bi, or landmine, the ninja reduced the number of his pursuers. He would lead them over prearranged patterns of these land mines, knowing that only he could be sure of the safe areas.

Warriors who sought to kill ninja with firearms were often foiled by the quick defense of the neru-kawa ito, a thick laminated leather protective shield behind which the contortionist ninja hid. Bullets would not penetrate that shield, or if they did, they rarely had enough shock power remaining to inflict a disabling injury.

## KARA-TE (EMPTY-HANDS)

Empty-handed combat, that performed without weapons, or while minimally armed, was a strong point in the ninja's skill. He trained himself in various methods of grappling with an enemy and also made use of the parts of his body to be used as weapons against the enemy's anatomical weakpoints. The ninja could deliver enough force by means of his fist, open hand, knee, head, or foot, to knock an enemy senseless. This skill had been developed from constant practice against wood, stone, and straw padding.

Many of the ninja's enemies wore protective body armor, in which cases assaulting techniques were less useful than grappling skills. The ninja was not impractical. In spite of the great skill he possessed he preferred to use weapons against his antagonist. The te kagi was primarily an instrument for climbing but could be used when worn on the hands to catch the enemy's blade and hold it helpless. With his other hand the ninja raked the spurs of the te kagi across the enemy's face. Sometimes he used ne-kade, which was also a climbing device, to get a better grip on the garments or flesh of his enemy before throwing him to the ground.

Iron bars sewn into the ninja's sleeves served as blocking surfaces against which the enemy's blade clashed harmlessly while the ninja counterattacked.

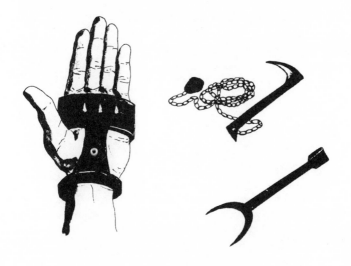

*Weapons and tools*

## CHAPTER 5

# TACTICS ... RUSES ... FEATS

The successful military commander knew that all warfare was based on deception. The actual physical clash of battle, put into its right perspective, must not precede effective espionage, that is, if victory was to be guaranteed. An indispensable preliminary to battle was an attack on the mind of the enemy. Ninja were the means by which a commander accomplished this important preliminary.

By use of ninja a commander frustrated his enemy's plans, broke up his alliances, created disharmony between superiors and inferiors, and in general, broke the enemy's will to resist. Intelligence was gathered by ninja who would simultaneously take advantage of every opportunity to sow the seeds of dissension, create false rumors, nurture subversion, and create confusion inside the enemy lines. All operations of the ninja were designed to demoralize the enemy.

Great care was taken by the ninja to select the point at which the enemy's ability to resist was weakest. By skillful avoidance or bypassing of the enemy's strong points the ninja would direct diversionary action against these strengths while actually breaching the weak points. All this had to be done in the shortest possible length of time and at the minimum cost of lives for the ninja's lord.

Most townspeople and many warriors believed the ninja to be sorcerers, or magicians who had gained mastery over nature. Their "occult" powers were spoken of in quiet, frightened whispers, and their suspected presence struck terror into the bravest of hearts.

Yet it was the ninja's personal resourcefulness, his dedication to his craft, his quick wittedness, and his remarkable physical toughness which made him appear to be super-human. He was simply a master of deception who used his tactics and specific ruses to throw the enemy into confusion while he carried out his assigned mission.

## THE KEY PRINCIPLES OF NINJUTSU

Deception and surprise were two key principles of the ninja. He attempted to lure the enemy into making false estimates and judgments which would lead to erroneous military actions. Always the ninja worked to deprive the foe of his superiority and initiative. When the enemy was united, the ninja divided him; where the enemy was unprepared, the ninja attacked him. The ninja knew how to keep the enemy under constant strain to wear him down.

With the enemy at ease, the ninja worked to weary him; with the enemy well provisioned, the ninja moved to starve him; when the enemy was at rest, the ninja attempted to rouse him into movement.

The ninja's sense of the timing of his probes against the enemy were acute. He appeared briefly at certain places and brought the enemy hurrying to combat him; then he moved swiftly out of sight and left a confused foe. At other times he struck in subtle ways which left no trace. He was inaudible, unseen, and mysterious, thereby greatly agitating the enemy who could not ascertain his pattern of movement. But he could be counted on to put the enemy in a desperate situation.

Some of the ninja's ruses were simple in nature, others more complicated, but all had their appropriate place in his bag of tricks. The ninja classified everything he did as either conforming to yo or positive techniques, that is, ones in which he would conceal himself by use of camouflage, or conforming to "in" or negative techniques in which he appeared in clear sight but in disguised form so that his true identity could not be discovered. He preferred to work alone, but under certain circumstances this was impractical and he became a member of a team.

Three major categories of ruses made his feats possible: (1) ruses for infiltration, (2) ruses for becoming "invisible," and (3) ruses for escaping.


## RUSES FOR INFILTRATING

It was basic to the success of every ninja's mission that he slip undetected into enemy territory so that he might go about the process of gathering intelligence, effecting arson, harassment, destruction or neutralization of the enemy's resources, or bringing off the deadly work of assassinating the enemy's leader.

After outfitting himself with the standard tools and weapons of his trade, the ninja usually arranged secret caches of other equipment and supplies which were necessary to sustain his operation in enemy territory. No preparation could be overlooked, for the slightest miscalculation would bring disaster upon himself and possibly his lord. Above all his journey into enemy territory had to be accomplished secretively.

To infiltrate enemy territory before hostilities erupted between the lord for which he worked and the enemy, a ninja might:

1. Seek out enemy warriors who were discontent with their lot and offer them rice wine, women, and money to betray their lord. Those who yielded to temptation would be a source of intelligence about the enemy's troop dispositions, logistics, and movements. But the ninja well knew that such traitors had to be carefully and continually watched so that they did not betray the ninja.

2. Obtain employment at a temple as a caretaker and work hard to get the head priest's recommendation to be transferred to the enemy lord's compound. Once assigned as a caretaker in the enemy lord's area, the ninja was in an ideal position to carry out intelligence missions or assassinate the enemy lord.

3. Become accepted by the enemy lord as a ninja in his service. The ninja would then accomplish meritorious work for his enemy employer and eventually disclose important facts about his real lord which enabled the enemy lord to gain some advantages. The enemy lord would commend the ninja, unaware that what had been done was but a carefully laid preparatory phase of a long-range plan to defeat him. The ninja would again give the enemy lord intelligence, but this time as hostilities broke out, the information would prove faulty and

the enemy lord's troops would be severely mauled in battle.

4. Use a beautiful woman to seduce an enemy lord. Some of the most valuable intelligence was gathered by this method from the intimacy of a lord's bed-chamber. However, the fact that some women actually fell in love with the lords they had expected to dupe could easily compromise this method, and it often became necessary for the ninja to kill the seductress.

5. Accompany dozens of other ninja who were each very obviously engaged in spying. As the enemy lord concentrated on rounding them up, the undetected ninja, operating in a sector removed from his companions, stood a good chance of succeeding in his mission.

6. Disguise himself as a traveler and feign sickness at the front gate of the enemy's compound. Enemy guards at the gate would by custom take the "sick" traveler inside the compound for treatment and rest, for it was a dishonor to have anyone die of sickness in front of a lord's gate. Once inside the compound the ninja would rapidly "recover" and leave. On the following day the ninja would return, asking and usually receiving permission to enter in order to thank the enemy lord for his kindness.

Inside the compound again the ninja this time would take every opportunity to make mental notes or sketches of the layout and might even find the chance to give his host the slip and go about his work unmolested. If discovered, the ninja would apologize for becoming "lost" in the confusion of a strange area.

The task of infiltrating enemy territory after hostilities between the enemy and the ninja's lord had begun was immensely more difficult and dangerous. The enemy would be extremely alert and overly sensitive to the possibility of ninja activity. But the ninja usually tried:

A. To ambush enemy troops camping for the night outside of their main area. Ambushes were particularly effective if the enemy troops had just concluded a long march; were bivouacked in heavy rain or snow; were bored from protracted confrontation; had just fought a heavy battle and were either regrouping for battle or were off guard because of their recent victory.

B. To slip unnoticed into the formations of the enemy about to return to their main base.

C. To allow himself to be captured after his escape plan had been readied. The ninja would have false information in written form on his person which if utilized by the enemy, would lead him into a well-set trap.

D. To mix with just-defeated enemy troops returning to their base. The ninja often assumed the role of a wounded warrior and once inside the enemy compound would be under less martial scrutiny and therefore much more free to go about his mission. He would, at the appropriate time, simply disappear from the area in which the wounded were quartered.

Inasmuch as every commander knew the strategic expediency of leaving some possible route of escape open to the trapped enemy, the besieged castle was one of the most difficult of all places for the ninja to infiltrate. The besieged commander well knew that any avenue of escape which he might devise was probably just as well known to his besieger;

to exploit such a possibility of escape was certainly to play into the enemy's hands.

Thus, under the threat of extinction, the besieged troops would offer their utmost resistance and the ninja who dared enter the besieged area became responsible for some of the most daring deeds of ninjutsu ever witnessed.

A ninja assigned this dangerous mission would wait for a moonless night or, that being impractical, the moment moon-masking clouds appeared, to make his entry. Also considered ideal conditions for such entry were rainy, windy, or snowy nights. Winter nights were risky, for though the cold might cause the enemy to huddle around fires or lull him into less watchfulness, the clear crisp air also served to carry the slightest sound and acted as a natural warning device.

The other seasons were also fraught with dangers, for though they were filled with natural noises of nature which tended to mask any noise the ninja might make, the interruption of these natural noises by the ninja would warn the enemy of an unwanted visitor's presence. But some conditions made for ideal times in which the ninja might make his entry:

1. The night some of the enemy warriors left the castle on a probing mission to find avenues of escape or were actually attempting to escape.

2. The night after the enemy had fought a severe daylight battle and sustained heavy casualties.

3. The night after the day in which the enemy had been unusually busy fortifying the castle.

4. The night the enemy was busy making preparations to take the offensive.

5. The night after the siege against the enemy had been lifted.

6. When the enemy became weary from long con-frontation.

7. When the enemy was struck with mass sickness, thirst, or hunger.

When the ninja moved to infiltrate a besieged castle, he had in mind to carry out systematic burning of fuel dumps, ammunition depots, armories and warehouses. Fires were to be lighted simultaneously so as to give the enemy the greatest possible difficulty in controlling them. This was accomplished by use of time fuses on incendiary devices or by the force of a team of ninja operating on a time schedule. Yet another purpose for making entry was to poison the enemy's food and water supply or simply to spoil his food and water with copious quantities of powerful purgative concoctions. No enemy fights well with an empty stomach, dry throat, or loose bowels.

# RUSES FOR INVISIBILITY

The ninja was no more able to make himself invisible than was any other human being, but he did such a good job at comouflage and applied such cunning ruses that for all practical purposes he operated as an "invisible" man. He became an unseen and insidious foe during the hours of darkness when nature contributed to concealing his movements and activities.

Darkness was the ninja's best friend; he worked well in pitch blackness for he was trained to do so. But when light appeared at the place where he must enter or work, the ninja took precautions against casting a telltale shadow. Silence, too, greatly aided the ninja's attempts to remain unseen, and on windy nights the ninja would attempt to work as much as possible in a position downwind from the enemy so that any sound inadvertently made would not easily carry to enemy ears.

Each tradition of ninjutsu had specific ruses, through the application of which it became famous, but ninja in general classified ruses for invisibility under four major headings: (1) ruses involving elements, (2) the heavens, (3) living forms, and (4) man-made objects or effects.

In the case of the elements the ninja made use of fire or light to blind the enemy, wood in the form of bushes or trees to camouflage himself, water to hide in or to screen his movements, and grass to hide in. The heavens provided the sky, fog, rain, moonlight, clouds, sun, lightning, thunder, wind, and snow, all of which had significance in ruses for making himself unseeable. Among living forms the ninja used women, children, aristocrats, peasants, birds, animals, fish, and even bugs as means of keeping the enemy from detecting his presence.

Man-made objects and effects such as buildings, statues, garden lanterns, and smoke also figured prominently in the ninja's ruses.

Some of the following ruses were particularly effective:

1. The ninja knew that a sentry who stared into a camp fire could not quickly accommodate his eyes to seeing into the dark. By creating a diversion in the fire . . . such as throwing a special kind of stone into it which popped and crackled loudly upon being heated . . . the ninja might get the sentry to watch the fire in an attempt to discover what was creating the disturbance. Then the ninja would make his move to by-pass the sentry.

2. Through the use of trees and shrubs to conceal himself the ninja advanced past sentries. Both immobile growth and foliage tied to the ninja's body were used.

77

*Ninja used trees and other natural growth
to mask their presence.*

3. Water in lakes, rivers, and moats could be used to hide in or to move noiselessly through by means of special swimming techniques, with or without a snorkle.

4. Terrain features such as defiles, draws, and defiladed areas provided the ninja a route into an enemy camp. By following these natural features the ninja could move undetected, especialy if he chose those regarded as impassable.

5. Two ninja, operating as a team, worked efficiently. While one caused some distracting noise, such as when pieces

of metal are clanged together, the other would, during the confusion, slip unseen into an enemy compound.

6. Deep grass was an excelent cover for movement, and additionally, if the wind was blowing in the right direction, the ninja might set the grass afire and use the combination of smoke and vegetation to conceal his activities.

7. Repetitive thunder and lightning often were severe enough to distract the enemy and let the ninja move past a critical point in the enemy's defense. Clouds obscuring the moon; fog, heavy rain or snow also worked to make the ninja an unseen and deadly agent. With the sun at his back in a clear sky -- if the ninja chose the right kind of background, no enemy looking in his direction would be able to observe him.

8. Human forms of the four different social classes (warrior, farmer, artisan, and merchant), provided a means by which a ninja in disguise might keep his identity concealed until he had drawn near to his objective. As darkness fell the ninja could shed his disguise and go about his insidious work.

9. Certain chemicals or even wet grass placed in fires which had been strategically located by the ninja gave out billows of smoke dense enough to screen his movements.

10. The ninja's many manners of walking served him in more ways than merely making him quick of foot. The peculiar side walking technique allowed him to pass through the narrowest of gaps between buildings which were rarely under scrutiny; with crab-like movements, back pressed close to one wall, the ninja went unobserved. Ceilings could be travrsed by use of special climbing tools, and in the darkness of a castle's corridors, the ninja lurking above went undetected.

Garden statues and stone lanterns could also be a ninja's salvation. By contortionistic manipulation of his body the ninja could imitate these objects and fool the enemy.

# RUSES FOR ESCAPING

Those ruses used to effect escape were closely related to those the ninja used for making himself "invisible." Largely the difference between them lay in the fact that after being observed the ninja more than likely would have to abandon his mission, at least temporarily, and make good his escape if he was to avoid capture. He was trained to take advantage of the slightest help from nature. As the enemy closed in on him, or in fact surrounded him, the ninja found the momentary effects of natural phenomena most useful.

For example, when the moon dipped behind a cloud, or when a gust of wind blew dust into the faces of the enemy, the ninja found it expedient to "disappear" or further confuse the enemy.

Six categories of the ruses that made ninja most difficult to capture were: (1) arboreal, (2) fire-flame-smoke, (3) aquatic, (4) metallic, (5) ground- object, and (6) living form.

When escape became necessary the ninja made use of arboreal ruses simply by running into dense foliage of bushes or trees, there to dodge animal-like in an unpredictable fashion so as to present an elusive target. Amidst the protective cover afforded by a bamboo grove, the narrow lanes made it difficult for masses of pursuers to follow the ninja; and it was usually impossible to bring long weapons into action. In the bamboo grove the ninja's method of walking sideways allowed him to move quickly through the labyrinth while his enemy became hopelessly bogged down in entangling brush.

To run away by using the distractions of light, smoke, and flame from inflammable mixtures as well as the effects produced by the noise of an explosion, was a favorite trick of the fleeing ninja. A puff of smoke, a flash of light from an exploding bomb tossed at the enemy usually created sufficient panic and confusion to make escape easy.

Aquatic ruses involved plunging into water to sit on the bottom for extended periods of time breathing through a snorkle tube; or the ninja could float along, just below the surface of murky water, as he clung to a weed bed, floating logs, or other debris, to safety. Even the keen scent of hounds sent to track the ninja would be foiled by this ruse. Metal rattled by a companion ninja located in a sector opposite to that in which escape was to be made, also distracted the enemy long enough to give the ninja an opportunity for escape.

Sand scooped from the ground and thrown in the eyes of the pursuing enemy or huge stones rolled down a slope hampered the enemy's ability to chase after the ninja. Specific ruses favored by ninja included:

1. As the enemy closed in, a ninja might leap into a tree under which he had carefully stationed himself after being discovered. The tree would be equipped with cables of vines or rope leading to some inaccessible place beyond the immediate vicinity of the tree. The ninja negotiated this distance quickly by means of swinging from the vines or by using his trolley equipment. With this advantage of a head start the ninja could easily outdistance his enemy.

2. A ninja might shine a light directly into the eyes of a single enemy who had come upon him suddenly. As the enemy reacted to the dazzling brightness, the ninja would move

away into the night. But a diversionary fire lighted opposite to the route of the ninja's planned escape was also useful in throwing the pursuer off track. And some cases were known in which the ninja played on the superstitious minds of his enemy. He wore a hideously carved mask of some demon or well-known evil spirit, and blew fire, from fire-works, from a tube to frighten and terrorize the enemy.

3. Often a ninja would simply throw some objects such as a heavy stone into a body of water as he hid along the bank. The enemy might believe that the ninja had dived into the water to hide, and would therefore occupy himself with searching the water area. The ninja then moved to safety overland.

4. When escaping townsfolk in particular, the ninja was known to throw quantities of metal coins at his pursuers. He threw perhaps to injure, but also to distract. While the townsfolk scrambled for the money, the ninja disappeared. Warriors, with their traditional disregard for money, were less prone to fall victim to this ruse. In such cases, the ninja would hurl his small throwing blades or caltrops to injure.

5. The ninja could hide like a fox in pre-made holes in the earth, covering himself with soil or other materials so that only his nose protruded; or he could bury himself deep in the earth and use his snorkle to breath air.

6. A ninja was trained to "give himself up as a human" and to become a part of some ground object. For example, he could imitate a stone or metal Buddhistic statue, a stone garden lantern, or could, by rolling up in a ball, "become" a stone on the landscape. Often he took a position in imitation of a scarecrow in a field, and so adept was he at this ruse that it was said that farmers often hung the garments on him as they went

about their chores. He blended with objects by clinging, face to the object, controlling his breathing, and restricting all movement to become inconspicuous.

The ninja was also skillful at tossing stones or pieces of wood in one direction to create a diversion. He would then escape in the opposite direction.

7. Ninja trained monkeys, dogs, snakes, lizards, crows, and rats to run into concentrations of people to serve as distractions, but in some cases animals were trained to fight against the enemy and delay him as the ninja took flight. A ninja on the run might dash into a crowd of townsfolk, there by quick change to disguise himself and mingle unnoticed with the crowd.

*The pursuit - a ninja escapes*

# THE MAGIC OF THE NINJA

The feats of ninja become less mysterious and awesome when his costume, tools and weapons, as well as his tactics and ruses are understood. But nevertheless, the ninja remained a remarkable person. While what he accomplished can be directly laid to his stupendous physical skills, acquired through years of hardships and brutal training in the apprenticeship of master ninja, it was the ninja's mental outlook which must also be understood.

In the preparation of his frame of mind prior to, during, and after embarking on a mission, the ninja demonstrated that he was in every sense of the word a religious man. Though he relied on his physical abilities to carry out specific actions, the ninja always offered prayers to gods and Buddhas as a means of summoning the resolution to perform dangerous deeds. He gained absolute confidence in himself by performing the kuju-kuri and simultaneously mumbling incantations, and then made use of the "in" signs to bind mental control.

The kuji-kuri was an important aspect of an ascetic practice known as Shugendo and also esotric Buddhism called Mikkyo. To perform kuji-kuri the ninja drew alternately five horizontal and four vertical lines in the air with a finger as he spoke mystic words; then he knitted his fingers together in puzzling patterns to make the "in" signs.

As reports of persons who had seen ninja perform skillful feats accumulated over the years, exaggerations of facts made the ninja out to be a superhuman. But the ninja was the last person to attempt to break his reputation. In fact, he thrived on making it even more remarkable than it was.

One of the most distorted impressions about ninja was that which accorded him the ability to jump unheard of heights and distances. While the ninja was perhaps without peer in such leaping, he nevertheless made use of implements to propel himself. Many a confused onlooker had seen a ninja leap to the top of a eight or nine foot garden wall or the eave of a low building, but in his excitement or fear had neglected to observe the device the ninja employed. A carefully concealed spring-board device located at the foot of the wall was powerful enough when jumped on to hurl the ninja upward and onto the wall. A length of cord was then used to haul the device up after the ninja to prevent its discovery.

*A ninja, disappearing in a cloud of smoke*

85

Great distances could be covered in one jump in the same manner, but here the ninja often used a clever acrobatic ricochet technique. Running at top speed, the ninja leapt against some stationary object such as a pole, tree, building, or stone. From this momentary touch-landing the ninja re-jumped the remaining distance and could cover upwards of 25 feet.

It was said that some mysterious medicinal concoction made from the vitals of horses enabled the ninja to be a great jumper and that the concoction was applied to the soles of his feet. But it is most doubtful whether any ninja really relief on such alleged power. Lengths of bamboo became useful as vaulting poles to carry the ninja over barriers 10 feet or more in height; similarly the ninja could leap great linear distances by this means.

Many a warrior attempting to capture a fleeing ninja ran into a clever trap known as the toketsu (rabbit den). The ninja dug a U-shaped tunnel along the path of flight. The larger end of this tunnel faced the direction from which the ninja would come, its opening being covered. Inside the tunnel the ninja place an oil mixture and an explosive charge.

The sides of the tunnel had been carefully lined with clay so that the oil mixture inside would not leak out. The explosive charges were placed to ignite the oil. A small fire would ignite the entire mass and explode it out the large end.

At the far narrow end of the tunnel the fleeing ninja or a companion waited to ignite the explosive mixture inside of the tunnel. The belch of flames was focused right into he faces of the pursuing enemy.

## PENETRATION TACTICS

A scaffold device called the yagora operated wheel-like fashion to hoist ninja to high positions such as might be necessary in forcing entry into a besieged castle. The device was moved under cover of darkness close to the castle wall. Ninja clung to huge spokes of the wheel which was turned by manpower from below. As the wheel revolved the topmost ninja would jump from the wheel onto the castle wall. Relays of ninja provided a means for multiple entries in this fashion.

The yami-dako (kite in darkness) was more of a psychological weapon and its method perhaps was never fully successful. A huge kite was sent aloft carrying a ninja who held fast to straps on its structure. When conditions were right, the ninja could be guided over enemy territory to remain aloft for surveillance, to fire at targets below, or to land silently to set about other missions.

Occasionally the enemy would be terrorized by huge kites on which figures of ninja had been drawn. These kites were usually flown as decoys for some other tactic being carried out by ninja in another sector of the enemy's territory.

*Mechanical flying device*

Yet another feat of the ninja was inspired by the eagle. In a technique known as hito washi (human eagle), the ninja tied himself to a glider device and was launched by the whip action of multiple bamboo poles which had been anchored in the ground. The top end of this launching device was winched down under forceful pressure exerted by a cable. When the bent bamboos were allowed to snap free, the glider with its ninja passenger would be lofted to soar a short distance into enemy territory.

Ninja ingenuity was responsible for the renpatsu suisha ho (repeating watermill gun), a device used to ascend to advantageous heights above a besieged castle's walls and deliver a volley of deadly gunfire or bombs. A huge wooden wheel, mounted on a carriage frame, could be rolled up and positioned near the castle wall where the thrust was to be made. The wheel had ten or more box-like compartments attached to its circumference.

Inside each of these boxes were two ninja-manned firearms. As the wheel revolved from man-power below, the boxes alternately came to the top of the wheel and provided the ninja with an elevation from which volleys of fire could be delivered against the castle. The time of revolution for the huge wheel to make one complete turn was such as to permit reloading at each gun position.

Ninja operated the toteki sha (throw wheel) against besieged positions. It was a battering ram designed to flatten walls, gates, and other structures of the enemy. A huge and heavy rock slung on a cable from a projecting arm on a moveable base was hauled back with a rope, then released to swing with great force against the chosen targt. The amplitude of the swing could be adjusted. Under continuous battering, the most solidly constructed defense eventually collapsed.

Another battering ram device was known as the kiko sha

(tortoise shell cart) which was also used in sieges. A heavy shield of cowhides which had been sewn together and stretched on a durable frame provided protection from arrows and other missiles. Under this protective canopy ninja activated a heavy wooden pestle held suspended on lengths of cable. By oscillating the pestle to and fro in a horizontal direction the exposed end of it could deliver a powerful blow against walls or gates.

An enemy position located in a deep and large valley could be invaded with terrifying speed and effect by means of the dai-sharin (big wheel). The daisharin was a cart which rolled on huge wooden wheels. Between the wheels rested a small cupola fitted with portholes through which the ninja could fire cannons and small arms, or toss bombs.

Many of these carts sent plunging down a hill into enemy concentrations wreaked havoc among the best-disciplined warriors and even if the warriors avoided the fusilade of fire, the heavy masses of the carts themselves were sure to crush substantial numbers of men, horses, and equipment.

## FUNA KAININ

The military feats of ninja were not limited to those on land. Ninja who operated on and under water and were assigned naval missions were known as funa kainin. One of the most sensational feats of the funa kainin was made possible by the ryu-o-sen (dragon boat). This boat was a submergible craft, which always operated under water except for its bow which was shaped in the form of a huge dragon. It was powered by paddle wheels operated under water from inside of the craft. Ballast was maintained by a carefully calculated cargo of sand bags, which when dumped allowed the boat to rise to normal flotation level.

Ninja operating inside the submerged craft could enter and leave it by means of a hatch in its bottom. The air supply was limited to just a few hours but was sufficient enough to enable the ninja to move close to the enemy fleet and attack. Using snorkle devices the ninja swam up under enemy hulls and drilled holes in them.

Other ninja invented the counter to the dragon boat. It was called the maruha-bune (round blade boat). A boat equipped with a pair of large circular saw blades travelled faster than did the submerged dragon boat and could approach the submergible almost without warning. Then fixed on a collision course with the dragon boat, the surface craft would move across and over the dragon boat and cut into it sufficiently to sink it. The fixed depth of the submergible made it unable to maneuver to avoid being thus cut in half.

# CHAPTER 6

# FACTS AND LEGENDS

Stories about the lives and exploits of ninja form a substantial portion of the aura of mystery which surrounds these masters of invisibility. Some of the stories are true. But a good many of them have become distorted by exaggeration, while still others are purely the result of persons with overly active and imaginative minds who have become possessed by the lure of ninjutsu.

The warrior, though trained to combat danger and to scorn death, could sometimes not help but fear the cunning and resourceful ninja whose accomplishments were on the lips of almost every townsman. The common people always feared the ninja, for their superstitious minds were the best targets for the propaganda of the ninja.

No ninja ever attempted to dispel the psychological advantage he gained over ordinary people by virtue of tales told about him. In fact, most ninja applied themselves energetically to the perpetuation of such stories or the addition of such new tales as would make them more terrifying to aristocrats and commoners alike.

Who, in feudal Japan, had not heard of Yamada Yaemon, a master of disguise, who could, it was said, change his person in such a large variety of ways and so quickly that he was able to move through a crowd of people and be remembered by them in a half-dozen or more different faces before he emerged from that crowd.

Kasumi Rosuke was famous for his clever slights and ruses. And Shimotsuge Kizaru, an expert in jumping techniques, jumped so well and so far that he literally appeared to those who chanced to see him in action to be flying through the air. Hachisuka Tenzo was famous for his ability to escape by digging through the earth. It was said that he could dig so quickly that no mole was a match for him.

## THE "MONKEY" NINJA

One of the most colorful ninja  was the lengendary Sarutobi Sasuke. Sarutobi, whose name meant "monkey jump," was famous for his monkey-like acrobatic skills and ferocious hand-to-hand fighting ability. Through the clever use of his body, Sarutobi was able to perform feats of running, jumping, and climbing normally possible only by monkeys. Sarutobi had trained himself diligently over a long period of years and excelled most ninja in physical condition. It is said that he even lived in trees, swinging and hanging, just as did the animals he was attempting to imitate.

The end result of his training made Sarutobi so nimble that no small group of persons, let alone a single man, could ever hope to capture this ninja in hand-to-hand combat. It was reported that Sarutobi could dodge the fastest warrior's blade, jumping above and ducking under its slashing arcs, or out of its range of thrusts, a procedure which usually brought the would-be captor to a state of rage and finally complete frustration. Then, laughing heartily, Sarutobi would scamper off and disappear.

Yet another aspect of Sarutobi was important. This concerned the quality of his loyalty and utter determination to serve his master. Sarutobi had been sent to spy on the Shogun (the milirary ruler of Japan) by his master who resided in a huge castle. Sarutobi's master and his followers had been declared rebels by the Shogun who had mustered his forces to effect the extinction of all such rebels.

Sarutobi had, however, made a successful entry into the Shogun's residence and had actually overheard secret plans being discussed by the military staff there. As he attempted to slip out of the Shogun's area, he was spotted by watchful guards who immediately gave chase. Sarutobi, who had experienced similar situations before, ran with confidence and cleverly eluded his pursuers, leaping onto a high wall surrounding the Shogun's residence by using a small springboard device which he had concealed alongside of the garden wall prior to final entry into the Shogun's private quarters.

Once atop the wall Sarutobi scampered quietly along its length and then jumped down on the far side . . . directly into a bear trap! As the Shogun's warriors closed in on him, Sarutobi cut off his own foot, just above the ankle, bound it with a tourniquet fashioned from the cord of his sword, picked up the severed foot and hobbled off. But Sarutobi had gone on his last mission. The extreme pain and the great loss of blood from the amputation was too severe a disadvantage for even the clever Sarutobi to offset.

*A ninja leaping down from a high castle wall.*

Standing on one leg, this courageous man shouted cries of defiance at his pursuers, then took his own life by the point of his sword which he ran completely through his neck to severe his jugular vein. The Shogun's guards, angry at not being able to take Sarutobi alive, rudely threw the dead ninja into the castle moat.


## THE SPEAR MASTER

Hattori Hanzo, a famous jonin ninja, was an expert with the spear. He likened the employment of that weapon with its fast thrusting attacks and speedy withdrawals to that of ninjutsu, in which it was necessary to strike quickly, then withdraw and disappear. The rule by which Hattori insured the success of all his operations was, "To deceive your enemy, first deceive your own side."

The death of Sarutobi gave Hattori cause to think of a scheme by which to further lull the rebels banding against the Shogun into a false sense of security and he ordered the news of Sarutobi's death to be kept secret. In the rebels' castle, everyone grew restless when Sarutobi failed to return or report. They dispatched a second ninja to contact Sarutobi and find out what was happening.

This ninja found the Shogun's palace under heavy guard, more than was normal, and so concluded that Sarutobi was operating in his usual style. This second ninja found entrance to the Shogun's palace a bit difficult but not unmanageable, never realizing that it had been conveniently arranged by Hattori for him to do so.

The rebel ninja was further allowed to overhear a conversation which told of the remarkable capture of Sarutobi and of his even more remarkable escape after he had presumably been killed and deposited for dead in the moat. Surely, as the rebel ninja observed, Sarutobi had managed to escape the Shogun's men, for there in the night before his very eyes, though he could not make personal contact with Sarutobi, was that monkey-like man moving stealthily up behind the Shogun's sentries. The rebel ninja watched as two of the guards were cut down and severely wounded.

The rebel ninja returned to his master's castle and there reported what he had observed. He made a recommendation that since the Shogun was under harassment by Sarutobi, the Shogun would be much too busy to launch a campaign against them. But almost before the ninja had finished his report, the Shogun's warriors encircled the rebels' castle and caught them off guard. When the castle finally fell a few days later, the remaining rebel survivors learned that Hattori had been too clever for them.

After Hattori had seen Sarutobi kill himself and had then disposed of his body, Hattori himself had taken the role of Sarutobi; working against his own men without them knowing about it. Hattori had confided his plan only to the Shogun.

# THE CARELESS NINJA

Kirigakure Saizo was a careless ninja. He trapped himself by a simple oversight. As he crouched silently one hot summer night under the floor of the residence of Kinoshita Tokichiro, a war lord he had been sent to spy upon, Kirigakure was suddenly stabbed through the shoulder by the accurate thrust of a spear penetrating downward through the floor above him.

Kirigakure had neglected to notice the unusual activity of the mosquitos which hummed noisily about him. But the lord's alert guards in the room above Kirigakure had not missed this important telltale sign which told of human presence below the floor. They had speared accurately and pinned Kirigakure to the ground where he was easily taken prisoner.

This account had an ironic twist. The fact that Kirigakure had failed to use mosquito repellent had actually saved his life, for a double agent, Takiguchi Yasuke, had been sent to kill Kirigakure and was about to do so when Kinoshita's guards speared the luckless ninja. Kirigakure's life was spared by Kinoshita on the condition that he declare loyalty to Kinoshita's cause.

## THE "TOILET" NINJA

Oda Nobunaga and Uesugi Kenshin were bitter enemies. Both had amassed considerable military power and were leaders of politically opposite causes. Ninja formed important portions of each leader's military might. Uesugi kept his security almost without flaw by trusting completely in the ability of Kasumi Danjo, a master of deception. Nevertheless the crafty ninja dispatched by Oda had managed to slip through Uesugi's outer guards and into that leader's private quarters. There they plotted Uesugi's destruction.

Ukifune Kenpachi, leader of the Oda ninja, was known for his accurate use of poison needles blown from his mouth. Hanging high above the dark corridor one night inside the Uesugi residence, Kenpachi and his ninja lured Kasumi Danjo and three Uesugi ninja into a trap. Kenpachi blew needles with vengeance and accuracy, and four bodies slumped to the floor. Kenpachi then moved rapidly to Uesugi's innermost room and prepared to assassinate his foe, but to his great surprise was set upon by Kasumi Danjo. Kenpachi suffered a painful beating at the hands of this strong ninja who dislocated Kenpachi's neck

97

and thus rendered him helpless.

Kasumi Danjo had only pretended to have been struck by the poisoned needle, and had feigned death as a counter ruse. Kasumi's three ninja, however, died from the poisoned needle.

As Uesugi relaxed and heaped praise upon Kasumi for work well done, he miscalculated the cunning of his rival Oda. Oda had foreseen a stalemate when he dispatched Kenpachi and had, therefore, really counted on using Kenpachi as bait. Secretly, Oda dispatched Ukifune Jinnai, who stood about three feet tall. It was this dwarf's mission to assassinate Uesugi. Ukifune's small stature came into good use on this mission.

In his training Ukifune had lived in a large earthenware jar, preparing himself for action in small cramped quarters. After

*The careless ninja*

98

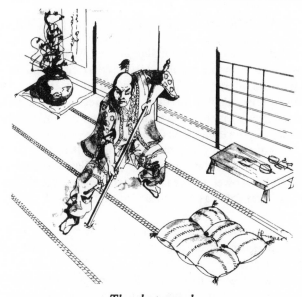

*The alert guard*

making entry into Uesugi's residence, Ukifune hid himself in the place where eventually Uesugi must come . . . the lavatory. As Ukifune hung in its lower recesses, he readied his short spear and had only to wait. Uesugi squatted in observance of his daily habit, and the dwarf thrust upward through Uesugi's anus, withdrew his spear, then burrowed into the fecal matter to escape detection by Kasumi Danjo and the rest of Uesugi's ninja and guards, who came rapidly onto the scene at the cries of pain from their dying master.

Ukifune breathed through a tube some inches below the surface of the lavatory cesspool. When the activity around the lavatory had ceased, Ukifune surfaced, slipped quietly from the lavatory, and made his way back to Oda to report his glorious deed.

# JAPAN'S MOST FAMOUS VENDETTA

Patience is a virtue essential to all successful ninja, and an unparalleled example of this virtue is to be found in the Chushingura, literally "A Treasury of Loyal Retainers," a true account of the slaying of Lord Kira. Because of a private quarrel, Lord Asano had drawn his sword and slashed at Kira-- a verbotten act--within the Shogun's palace.

By order of the Shogun, Asano committed hara-kiri that same night, whereupon forty-seven of his Samurai retainers-- led by Oishi--vowed to wreak vengeance on Lord Kira, whom they justly regarded as the cause of the quarrel with their dead master.

Kira, however, suspected that the now-masterless Samurai (called ronin) might do just that, so he set his own ninja to watching them.

To allay these suspicions, Oishi and the other forty-six ronin spread out over the countryside and took jobs as carpenters, smiths, merchants, etc. professing to have no further interest in the cause of their late lord. Oishi himself went to Kyoto where he energeticaly threw himself into a deliberate program of drunken debauchry, spending many nights in the gutter, later abandoning his wife and children for the company of a sturdy harlot.

After gaining experience in such menial employment as cooks and gardeners in other areas, several of the ronin were eventually able to get jobs within Kira's mansion itself.

Even before this, however, others of the ronin had once deliberately set a fire along the outer wall surrounding Kira's extensive holdings. Taking advantage of the confusion and the rush to extinguish the flames, these ronin infiltrated Kira's bastion and, mounting to the tops of such coigns of vantage as roofs, trees, and towers, rapidly sketched the interior intricacies of its labyrinthine corridors and twisting garden paths.

Although Asano had committed hara-kiri in April, 1701, the forty-seven ronin managed to suppress their burning rage for revenge and bided their time until January of 1703, by which time Kira had concluded no harm would come from such as they, and recalled his own watchful ninja whom he set to other tasks.

In January, 1703, Oishi decided that all was ready for the final act of the greatest vendetta in Japanese history. Making the long journey from Kyoto to Edo, he called his forty-six co-conspirators together and then, in the best ninja tradition, waited for a favorable turn in the weather.

What was considered good weather by a ninja was, of course, not always so regarded by others. So it was on the 30th of January--twenty-one months after Asano's self-disembowlment--that Oishi decided to take action--on a night when most others were huddled over charcoal braziers or half-tucked in warm kotatsu heating pits.

Outside a blizzard raged, rattling shutters, muffling the sounds of intrusion, and reducing visibility to nearly naught. With aid of the wild snow-storm and using the knowledge gained by their ninja tactics, Oishi and his long-patient band broke into Kira's mansion, cut down his followers, and at length discovered Kira himself cowering in a small outhouse.

True to the code of Bushido, they first offered the object of their hatred the chance to commit hara-kiri himself, this being a more honorable way of death than simple execution. But Kira evidently did not have the courage to cut himself open, so his head was lopped off and carried in a procession to the cemetery on the grounds of the Sengakuji Temple (in the Takanawa district of what is now Tokyo) and there laid before the grave of Lord Asano.

While many of the populace and even the great Daimyo (lords) applauded the successful revenge and extolled the patience with which it was planned and executed, the killing of Kira was nonetheless a violation of the stern Tokugawa code, so all forty-seven ronin were ordered to commit hara-kiri. This they did with outstanding equanimity. They were buried with their lord and are still revered as heroes by a great many of their fellow countrymen.

## THE RAT MANURE FOIL

Feigned sleep fooled very few ninja. Sandaifu Momochi always slept lightly, for he feared the ninja of his arch-enemy Takeda Shingen. Hajika Jubei, a ninja who had been dispatched by Takeda to kill Sandaifu, had silently entered Sandaifu's residence and lurked in the dark waiting his chance to complete his assigned mission.

Upon locating Sandaifu, apparently deep in slumber, Hajika released several hungry weasels that had been starved for many days and had become very vicious. Hajika then prepared to blow poisoned needles into Sandaifu to ensure the death of his wily victim, but before he could carry out his plan the crafty Sandaifu heaved a bag of rat manure onto him. Weasels are greatly attracted to rat manure and therefore left the intended victim, Sandaifu, for Hajika, who died of their bites.

## AVOIDING POISON

Sampo Jinzai was a skillful and resourceful ninja. A Tokugawa ninja, dispatched to kill Jinzai, failed to carry out his mission because of Jinzai's alertness. It happened that Jinzai had occasion to take refreshment at a roadside inn. Unknown to him, the Tokugawa ninja, who had been following him, had been able to poison the water supply from which tea was made and also to add some equally deadly poison to the supply of bean-cakes which Jinzai had ordered. The unsuspecting innkeeper placed the tea and poisoned cakes before Jinzai and then left to go about his chores.

As Jinzai was about to drink his tea, he noticed the slight cloudiness of the beverage, a feature of poisoned liquid. Jinzai threw the contents of the cup into a small fish pond near where he sat, and in short order several of the fish turned belly up. Jinzai then examined the bean-cakes before him. They had small beads of moisture on their surfaces, another sure sign of poison. To be certain, Jinzai cruelly threw one to a cat sunning itself near his table. The cat, within minutes of eating the cake, rolled over in agony and died.

Summoning the waiter, Jinzai paid his bill and left with polite excuses for not finishing the second cake or ordering more, for he knew that the poisoning had been the work of some enemy ninja. No local citizen would have the ability to concoct such a deadly poison.

# THE DEATH OF LORD KUWANA

Not all war lords could devise enough security to make their residence impervious to the ninja. The lord of Kuwana was a neat and orderly man, an aristocrat who enjoyed epicurean pleasures. Wise in the ways of the ninja, this lord had always been successful in negating their best efforts to kill him, for to take such a high official's life would be a singular honor for any ninja serving the lord's enemies.

The lord of Kuwana had made elaborate arrangements to

detect and trap ninja. He often boasted that no ninja could enter his domain without his knowledge. He had posted double sentries, and kept dozens of wild dogs continually on the prowl around the gardens of his palatial residence.

Additionally, all sorts of ingenious devices installed within his residence proper trapped any intruders. Deep wells had been dug in strategic places under the floors of corridors. The flooring could be set to be triggered by the weight of a man's body and the intruder who walked on such floors would then be dumped into the well beneath where he would be at the mercy of the guards. Secret suspension devices had been installed and could be activated to tip certain rooms at an angle which would hurtle all occupants of such rooms into one corner, unable to stand or escape.

In yet another guest room, water could be made to fill the garden area which surrounded it. The garden actually formed the perimeter of a moat around the room. Occupants in the special room would soon find themselves trapped by the rising water. Archers and spearsmen on the perimeter of the wall surrounding the room could bring quick destruction to all occupants.

At night the lord of Kuwana slept in splendor. He lounged in luxurious silks on a magnificent bed placed in the precise center of the room. This arrangement was made to allow the lord to enjoy the painting on the ceiling which had been specially done by a skilled artist of the times with no expense spared. The lord dearly loved to stretch out under the painting and let its aesthetic qualities lull him to sleep. Once he had ordered a chambermaid killed for arranging his bed just off center.

More than one ninja had attempted to kill the lord of Kuwana. All had failed, and those who had not had the

*A ninja prepares to descend into a room from the attic*

foresight to kill themselves were tortured unmercifully. Totsuka Jiro, a lad of five, had lost his famous ninja father to the lord of Kuwana's cunning. The elder Totsuka had triggered one of the floors and had been dumped into the well under the floor. Captured alive, the elder Totsuka suffered great pain as the lord of Kuwana's guards peeled off his skin, bit by bit. Jiro had never forgotten the incident and vowed to avenge the death of his father and restore the honor of his family and his ninja tradition.

For two years the tiny lad surveyed the Kuwana domains, gathering such intelligence as he could glean from overhearing the talk of guards and listening to those who had been invited guests within the great walls. Gradually the small assorted bits of information fitted together and at last Jiro was able to devise a clever scheme for entering the domains and killing the dreaded and haughty lord.

The youngest son of the lord of Kuwana had befriended Jiro and often took Jiro inside the Kuwana estate. Jiro's trained eye missed nothing as his young host eagerly and proudly pointed out the many traps which had been rigged to trap ninja. Jiro's keen eyes did not betray his true feelings as on one occasion he actually met the lord of Kuwana as he and his playmate amused themselves at children's games in front of the Kuwana residence. Jiro, however, was only awaiting his chance. That chance came one afternoon as his playmate went to his quarters in search of more toys. Upon his return he found Jiro gone and concluded that his friend had become bored and left.

But Jiro had not left the Kuwana grounds. He had hidden himself in an old abandoned well, supporting himself with a special sling of unbreakable line which he always carried on his person. That night, as the lord of Kuwana slept in his magnificent chamber and was well under the spell of the painting high on the ceiling directly over him, young Jiro walked noiselessly down the corridors without fear that his slight bodyweight would trigger the traps; his young friend had taught him such useful knowledge.

Jiro hoisted himself quietly into the rafters above and behind the ceiling of the room in which the lord of Kuwana slept, then began his clever plan to end the life of the man who had ordered his father killed.

Jiro first drilled a small hole in the ceiling. Peering down through it he could just make out the form of the lord sprawling on the bed, and he went about the next step of his plan. He unwound a length of strong silk string and fed it down just a few inches from the sleeping lord's face. Then Jiro waited. At midnight the lord broke into a heavy snore, mouth agape.

106

Jiro quickly opened a vial he was carrying, dipped a small stick into the poisonous liquid within the vial, and placed a few drops on the string which dangled from the ceiling. The liquid slowly slid down the length of string and when it reached the end dropped directly into the lord's open mouth. Jiro waited no longer than to hear the cries of pain uttered by the lord. He picked up his gear and retraced his steps out of the residence into the outer compound.

The lord of Kuwana fumed and gagged as the poison worked into his system. In short order he died. His guards frantically searched the room for evidence of who had killed him and how. In the confusion caused by the mysterious assassination, Jiro slipped by the guards and over the outer wall to freedom. He had avenged the death of his father and could now return to his family and ninjutsu tradition.

## THE "DEATH" OF A NINJA

Kaei Juzo, a ninja, lived under daily threat of being killed by Tokugawa ninja. As coincidence would have it, Tonbe, a former ninja partner of his, worked for the Tokugawa Shogunate. Upon preparing to kill Juzo, Tonbe recognized his old friend and could not carry out his mission. The two agreed to a plan which would enable both of them to at least nominally have a chance to please their masters.

Tonbe led Juzo back to the Tokugawa headquarters, declaring Juzo to be his prisoner. As was expected the Shogun ordered Juzo killed. Juzo pleaded that he be allowed to take his own life and the Shogun, curious as to how a ninja accomplished suicide, granted the plea. As Juzo knelt before the Shogun to display his method of suicide, he was seen to plunge a small knife into his abdomen. Blood soon soaked his garments and then slowly Juzo tipped forward and fell on his face. The Shogun, satisfied, ordered Juzo's body dumped into the moat.

That night Juzo came back into the Shogun's castle and harassed the Tokugawa by means of arson. The crafty Juzo had used his opportunity at audience with the Shogun to mentally map important details of the inner compound. He had merely plunged the knife into the body of a small, freshly killed animal which lay concealed under his garments; it was the animal's blood which had stained Juzo's garments and led all, including the Shogun, to believe Juzo had committed suicide.

## THE IMPREGNABLE CASTLES

The castle at Mino was well known as an example of a ninja-proof structure. No successful penetration by ninja had ever been accomplished, and the lord of the castle boasted that his fortress was impregnable. Its outer stone wall looked down commandingly upon the murky water of the moat surrounding it. The wall itself was, perhaps, scalable, but such action would not go undetected, for every inch of the wall was under the constant scrutiny of highly trained and alert guards who were located in special watch towers atop each corner of the wall. Yet Koga ninja managed to enter the castle by scaling those walls right under the eyes of the sentries and to wreak havoc among the castle's occupants.

On the night of a great August typhoon, heavy winds whipped the falling rain downward at such an angle that the view on the windward side from one of the watch towers was obscured. The Koga ninja took advantage of this fact, swam the moat, scaled the wall, did their work within the castle undetected, then returned to safety all while the typhoon raged furiously around them. Sentries in the guard towers, though they did not relax their vigil, had felt secure behind the fury of the elements.

Although the guards had been physically unable to keep the small section of the wall under surveillance due to the downbeating rain, all committed suicide in atonement for their failure to maintain the security of the castle.

Ninja were especially receptive to challenges offered by castles which defied surreptitious entry. The castle at Suwa had only one guard tower, but because that tower was positioned higher than the surrounding wall and interior structures and because it commanded a view of the entire internal compound of the castle, the castle was regarded as entry-proof. Ninja knew that unless this one tower could be neutralized no successful penetration could be sustained, but Kato Tanzo of Iga was an ambitious ninja. He planned to take control of Suwa castle and establish himself as lord and master of that fortress. Although scaling the Suwa castle wall was an ordinary feat, especially on the moonless night which Kato chose to bring off his plan, the capture of the guard tower was a challenge to his imagination.

Kato himself climbed the castle wall directly under the guard tower. This was a blind spot in the castle's defense, which Kato had spotted from his long study of the features of the castle. From his precarious position Kato drilled a small hole in the overhanging floor portion of the tower. That accomplished, Kato quietly inserted an expanding bolt into the hole. This was fixed into position by unlocking its expandable head, which was larger than the diameter of the hole which accommodated its shaft.

Thus, as the four guards inside the watch tower kept their usual vigil, this operation actually took place right under their feet. Kato then repeated a similar operation some distance away from the first hole. From these bolts, Kato strung a special sling and rigged a small platform. He then signaled to four ninja waiting in the murky water below to join him.

*A ninja cuts down a foe*

The five ninja then hung above the moat in the darkness, right under the very feet of their foes. From this position it was an easy matter for them to climb the remaining few feet and slip in on the sentries unnoticed, kill them, and thus gain control of the watch tower which commanded the castle. Then arson against the castle was carried out in a matter of minutes.

## THE NINJA WHO WALKED ON WATER

Saji Gorobei was a ninja who was highly skilled at feats of crossing water by means of flotation devices. He had successfully negotiated some of the most treacherous strips of water, those filled with whirlpools, eddies, and strong undercurrents.

Saji and his small band of ninja were operating in the Lord of Bingo's area, some fifty miles from their base ninja camp. They had uncovered valuable intelligence about the enemy at Bingo, but now needed to transmit it to their leader at the base camp.

Unfortunately, their operations had been detected by alert guards who had discovered signs of espionage activity. One of Saji's ninja had unavoidably left some tell-tale puncture marks with his climbing instruments on the huge trees which surrounded the Lord of Bingo's inner compound. The whole area now bristled with warriors. The Lord of Bingo, sensing the danger of ninja operating against him, had ordered all roads leading out of Bingo placed under surveillance.

Saji dispatched fellow ninja Yamaguchi Yaemon, who before long was caught by the Bingo warriors. But Yaemon died loyal to his ninja tradition. As the Bingo warriors closed in on him, he disfigured his face with the point of his sword so that his captors could not identify him. Another ninja, Komori

111

Mataemon, was dispatched to attempt transmittal of the important intelligence to the base camp. Komori was a master of disguises, but he too was trapped by the alert warriors of Bingo. The ninja, disguised as an itinrant priest, was walking directly along one of the major roads leading out of Bingo. It was a daring plan, for the ninja had to walk through hundreds of the enemy who roamed the roads.

All was going well until a suspicious warrior moved his spear to a threatening position and ordered the priest to give him a benediction. Komori's skill at disguises did not stop with the external trappings. He had also mastered the various skills of the persons he imitated. Without flaw Komori uttered a pious benediction for his threatening host and was so convincing that the warrior actually gave him alms.

Komori walked through a small village, just beyond which was the last barrier gate and the road to freedom outside of Bingo. A runaway oxcart suddenly appeared at a turn in the road and was headed straight at Komori. The ninja nimbly dodged the cart by leaping over the backs of the oxen . . . much too skillfully for an ordinary itinerant priest.

The Bingo warriors were on Komori like a flash, cutting him down quickly with their razor-sharp swords.

Saji was desperate. The need to transmit the important intelligence was more pressing than ever. His small band of ninja had been reduced by two. That night he conceived a daring plan. Under cover of darkness, he slipped quietly down to the seashore. The Bingo coast was one of the most treacherous in Japan. No craft ventured too close to its shores, fearing the various currents and many reefs which dotted the approaches to the beaches. Even the feared wako, the corsairs who sailed boldly from Japan to Korea and the southern Chinese coasts, avoided the Bingo shores. Saji knew that for these reasons Bingo security was practically non-existent in

112

that area.

Saji waited patiently in the scrub brush on the water's edge. At ebb-tide he slipped noiselessly into the water with his strange equipment, portable flotation devices called mizugumo (water spiders). After he had drifted out to sea and was invisible from the shore, Saji fastened the mizugumo to his feet and walked until just before sunup, then came ashore in friendly territory, from which going back to his base camp was an easy task.

## THE NINJA SUBMARINERS

Those ninja trained in naval espionage, the fuma kainin, had harassed the Tokugawa government for many years. They roamed without fear of capture or suppression in the Inland Sea area. One of their leaders, Fuma Kotaro, was particularly effective in striking against the Tokugawa installations and was causing irreparable damage. In desperation the Tokugawa government called upon Hattori Hanzo to bring an end to the menace of the fuma kainin. Fuma Kotaro was especially wanted . . . dead or alive.

Hattori ordered the construction of dozens of large boats. These boats were equipped with heavy guns. Hattori knew that the fuma kainin had but few craft; all were small and had practically no armament at all. When the fleet was ready, Hattori ordered it to scour the Inland Sea areas and to destroy all the fuma kainin craft and their dreaded occupants. Off the Suo coast the Tokugawa gunboats came upon a small group of craft of the fuma kainin. The Tokugawa gunboats maneuvered to get within volley distance, then laid down a steady and heavy barrage.

One by one the small craft of the fuma kainin were struck

and took fire, except one, which had remained well out of gun range. This boat made no attempt to sail away, and appeared to be floating helplessly unable to further distance itself from the punishing naval barrage laid down by the Tokugawa gunners.

Hattori ordered his gunboats to move slowly toward their target so that a concerted broadside could be fired to finish off the craft which by now burned vigorously. As the Tokugawa gunboats drew close, the tide shifted and both the fuma kainin craft and the Tokugawa gunboats were being sucked into a narrow channel.

Hattori gave the command to maneuver to avoid collision. A frantic cry from his helmsman was repeated on each and every gunboat of the Tokugawa: "No rudder!" The Tokugawa boats were without steering gear and the burning craft of the fuma kainin slid rapidly toward them threatening to set the whole Tokugawa fleet afire. Hattori sensed the great danger and ordered the powder magazines dumped into the ocean, but there was no time to complete this action.

Instead, the Tokugawa sailors and Hattori himself abandoned ship. The fuma kainin had prepared for just such an eventuality, for as the Tokugawa men splashed about in the water they realized that its surface was covered with oil! In seconds the entire surface of the ocean was turned into a blazing inferno.

Fuma Kotaro stood calmly on the deck of his command craft, the one which had not ventured too close to the scene. His underwater ninja had done their job well, for while the Tokugawa ships were manuevering in close prior to attempting their broadside, his ninja had swam in under their boats and disconnected their rudders.

# SODOMY AND THE SECRET DOCUMENT

There was a certain manuscript, a Chinese classic, which was highly prized by military commanders, could they but obtain it. The only copy of the manuscript was in the hands of, and jealously guarded by, the head abbot of Kumano.

The manuscript was reported to make military geniuses out of all who mastered its contents. It was said that its compiler, a Chinese general, was able to nock eight arrows at one time and to launch them simultaneously to strike down eight enemy, all because of this miraculous text.

Kozuke Morinao was a rash warrior. He had spared no expense in attempting to obtain the Chinese classic but had always failed. The monks of Kumano were watchful, guarding their abbot's prized possession with meticulous care. Kozuke thus sent his top ninja, Horikawa Genzo, to the Kumano temple complex with instructions to locate the secret repository in which the classic was kept.

Horikawa made his surveillance in the guise of a monk, a role which he had spent countless hours studying in preparation for this mission. But try as he might, Horikawa could not discover where the manuscript was hidden. He discreetly questioned follow monks about the manuscript but could get absolutely no information.

However, Korikawa noticed a small building in the main temple compound which was kept under constant guard. Between four and six o'clock in the afternoon the guard force was changed. Individual guards were posted at irregular hours, a procedure which made a regular pattern impossible.

Upon further questioning Korikawa learned that this was the private treasury of the Kumano temple and contained not only their supply of money but priceless art objects as well.

115

Surely, thought Horikawa, this was the logical place for the manuscript to be stored.

No plan which Horikawa entertained seemed to have a chance for success, except the idea of tunneling up under the storehouse. Horikawa spent some seven months digging a tunnel, always working quietly at night. He began his shaft from a dense clump of brush which bordered on a fast-moving stream running through the temple grounds. The earth which Horikawa removed from the tunnel was thus easily disposed of in the stream where the flow of water washed it away.

One night as Horikawa dug, his calculations told him that he was soon to break through under the storehouse. When his digging tools struck something solid, he was greatly joyed. But his joy was short-lived, for he discovered that he had struck solid rock. For three more months Horikawa labored, only to find that the entire floor of the storehouse rested on a huge rock. His best efforts proved that it was impenetrable.

The story had an ironic ending for Horikawa, for unknown to him the head abbot had discovered the tunnel and had allowed Horikawa to dig unmolested. On this, the last night, the abbot ordered a huge fire built at the entrance to the tunnel. Wet weeds and grass were piled on the flames and billows of dense smoke rose into the air. A group of monks fanned the smoke into the tunnel. Inside, as the choking smoke reached him, Horikawa tried frantically to dig an escape route, but was suffocated before he could do so.

When Horikawa failed to return after a year's absence, Kozuke sent another ninja to investigate the situation. From that ninja Kozuke learned that Horikawa had been discovered and killed. Kozuke schemed for many weeks thereafter until at last he devised a plan which he was certain would succeed.

Eda Hachiro was a young teenage ninja, handsome and

116

trained as a dancer and musician. Eda was to be sent into the Kumano compound in the role of a chigo, a page. Chigo were lavishly dressed by the monks and used in homosexual activities.

Eda faced his assignment without demur and through his youthful grace and beauty soon gained the attentions of the head abbot who had him transferred to his private quarters. Eda danced daily for the head abbot and eventually became sexually intimate with him. But the young ninja dared not question the abbot about the manuscript, for to do so would surely arouse suspicion.

Eda then struck up a friendship as a part-time chigo for an assistant abbot who was very jealous of the head abbot's attentions toward Eda. From this assistant abbot Eda learned that the Chinese classic was always on the head abbot's person.

One afternoon as the head abbot bathed to prepare himself for his amorous activities with his chigo, Eda had the opportunity to search the abbot's clothes for the priceless document. He found nothing. Peering in at the abbot in his bath, Eda spotted a small cylindrical metal tube at the edge of the bath . . . It had to be the manuscript!

Eda also learned from the assistant abbot that the head abbot never opened the container except at night in the dim light of a candle or oil lamp which was turned down. His study of the document was always confined to the hours of darkness, supposedly when no peering eyes could hope to share its contents. Eda made up his mind to kill the head abbot and to make off with the cylindrical tube and thus bring to a speedy end this mission which had always been repulsive to him.

That night, as the head abbot studied the Chinese classic, Eda slipped silently into the room behind the abbot and garotted him with a short length of chain. Taking the document, Eda then carefully made his way out of the Kumano compound and back to his master, Kozuke.

Kozuke was over-joyed. Greedily he snatched the container from Eda's hands, chased his faithful ninja from the room as Eda mumbled something about the tube always being opened only in semi-darkness. Kozuke paid no heed to such mumblings and excitedly spread the manuscript on a low table before him in the sunlight of his small room. With trembling hands Kozuke adjusted the manuscript and began reading its precious contents.

Before he had finished the opening paragraphs, Kozuke flew into a rage, for these words told him that the manuscript must never be opened in bright light to avoid obliterating its text. The Chinese general had written the entire contents, other than the introductory paragraph, in a special kind of ink which would obliterate itself in sunlight!

## THE NINJA IN BATTLE

Kusunoki Masashige was a military genius, a man so gifted that it was commonly said that he schemed in his tent ten thousand leagues from the battlefield and from such a remote point could engineer a victory. Kusunoki well appreciated the value of ninja, for many of his successes had depended upon the use of these super sleuths.

Kusunoki had founded his own ninjutsu troop which was primarily concerned with tactical deployment on the battlefield. Because he understood the work of the ninja so well, Kusunoki had spent countless hours devising what he considered a ninja-proof method by which tactical plans could be formulated without fear of compromise. This method was simple, yet no counter-ninja activity ever succeeded in breaking Kusunoki's security.

118

*Ceiling-clinging technique*

Kusunoki and his top military commanders would always meet at a prearranged location. It made little difference whether the meeting was held outdoors or inside. At times the battlefield was used, while at other times under less urgent circumstances, a farm house or more substantial residence was utilized. The meetings could be held in broad daylight or at night. If the latter, the dim light of a small fire illuminated the proceedings.

Kusunoki and his commanders would crouch around a stone tablet. Not a single sound would be uttered. Instead, the precise details of the plan would be spelled out by tracing the written characters in a light coating of fine ash which Kusunoki

119

sprinkled on the slab. Each commander would either nod his approval or trace his counter-ideas in the ashes. When agreement had been reached, the final plan would be written, a few phrases at a time, so that each commander could memorize it. Then the knowledge of what had transpired remained only in the minds of Kusunoki and his commanders.

The loyalist cause in defense of Chihaya Castle (near modern-day Osaka) against the Hojo commanders owed its success to the martial resourcefulness of Kusunoki. Kusunoki had fought a brilliant series of delaying actions which he designed to give himself time to properly fortify Chihaya. His main purpose was to bring the final battle into terrain where the Hojo's superior numbers would not be of much advantage.

Chihaya stood atop high ground near the summit of Mount Kongo, and the surrounding terrain features were well known to Kusunoki, but not to his attackers. Behind the castle's walls, Kusunoki and his resolute warriors fought skillfully, secure with an adequate food and water supply.

Great boulders were placed so that they could be dropped or rolled down on the attackers. Huge brushwork emplacements were erected to deflect arrows, and the attackers found it impossible to deploy cavalry and large numbers of troops against the fortress.

Kusunoki directed the preparation of huge wooden vats which were then filled with human excreta. These vats were balanced precariously at strategic points on the castle walls. When some of the attackers were so lucky as to penetrate Chihaya's outer perimeter defenses, they were met with a stream of foul-smelling slurry mixture that so thoroughly covered the walls and the base of the castle that the would-be invaders had no stomach for attacking at close quarters.

Not all ninja remained attached to a life of service with their original groups. Some individuals and groups broke their organizational ties and operated separately as robbers, plunderers, or even corsairs. The fuma kainin were particularly notorious for such independent actions. They plied the Inland Sea areas in their dragon boats (ryu o sen), stealing what they could from the coastal villages in order to build a logistic base. Their booty and its caches were not easily discovered. An inquisitive fisherboy was responsible for uncovering the secret of Awaji Island.

One of the most mysterious of all dragon boats operated around Awaji Island. Villagers on the mainland were being terrorized by a huge monster- headed boat which appeared to actually be a live dragon. It would swoop down on coastal inhabitants without any warning, smoke belching from its ugly maw. Though the villagers never ventured close to the beast-like craft, many fishermen who were afloat when it appeared swore that it would, after completing its raid, move around one tip of Awaji Island and just disappear. Observers aboard government gunboats sent in chase made similar reports. While commoners and government warriors shook their heads in disbelief, the ninja responsible for the use of the dragon boat plotted still more raids, safe behind the security of a clever facade.

The head of the dragon, located at the prow of the craft, was large enough to be used as a lookout post for navigational purposes. A small controlled fire could be kindled inside the head to keep the lookout warm in cold weather, but could also be used to produce smoke and create the effect of the dragon breathing smoke.

At one end of Awaji Island there was a promontory with sheer cliff facings. One side of these cliffs featured a low-arched cave entrance barely noticeable from the sea side even at low tide. Because it was so small nobody had ventured to

121

investigate it until one day a young lad who was fishing near the cliff happened to wash in close to the low-arched opening at the water's level. He found that he could just manage to slip his small dinghy through the opening.

What he saw on the other side made him depart in a hurried retreat. On the mainland he reported what he had discovered to his father, who in turn told the commandant of the warrior detachment stationed in the village. It was not too long before a sizable government naval force arrived on the scene and the secret of Awaji Island came to an end.

The fuma kainin who operated the dragon boat of Awaji Island had precise knowledge of the tides. All raids were carefully timed with the rising tide. As the dragon boat completed its mission and moved around the promontory at Awaji Island, the low-arched cave entrance disappeared, but the ninja knew accurately where it was located. They aimed their dragon boat right at this unseen entrance. Travelling at a partially submerged depth, the dragon boat would appear to any observers to actually sail right into the sheer cliff wall and disappear.

What was actually happening was that it passed through a sizable entrance which lay beneath the surface of the water into a huge cave which was large enough to act as a dock for the dragon boat and a logistic base for the ninja.

# DEATH OF A FOOLISH WARRIOR

For several hours now you have been mentally reviewing all you know about ninja and their deadly skills. You were foolish to let yourself doubt your ability to deal with them. The review has been good for you, for now you are greatly relieved and the fear which shamed you earlier has subsided. Only a few more minutes and you will be relieved of duty.

In your report to the commandant, you will, naturally, neglect to mention the shameful fear that seized you.

A bat flits by and you catch the swiftness of its erratic flight in the light of the moon, which even in its dimness has actually been rather friendly. Then, suddenly, the moon slips behind a thick cover of dark clouds and you are left in almost total blackness . . . a miserable way to end a watch, you think. Then you break off your thoughts about the moon and clouds, for there is an omnious silence.

The silence rings loud in your ears. Your blood pounds in your temples as your pulse quickens . . . Silence can be deafening to the supersensitive warning system of a successful, professional warrior such as yourself. It is trying to tell you something.

Something is wrong, very wrong. But what is it? Yes, that's it! The frogs in the moat! They've stopped their noise . . ! But no, there they go again, so perhaps it was your imagination.

But now . . . there is something else . . . something else

very wrong. The crickets! That's it! The crickets have stopped chirping their merry melodies from the chinks in the stone wall which rises up from the moat!

These are warning signals to be sure, and your fighting instincts are now fully aroused. You are not alone. You hand trembles as it reaches for your sword, for now fear is back once again to give you miserable company.

Fear? Yes. You know you are not alone, but who? Where? This infernal blackness! And fear . . . fear that penetrates to the marrow of your bones.

But it would be foolish to sound the alarm, to alert the other guards, for a brave warrior such as yourself must deal with the situation alone. You would be the target of great ridicule and dishonor should it prove to be nothing at all, or simply the work of one brave enemy.

So you will not give the alarm. You will finish your watch in honor. This is your decision and you know that it is the only one you can make and keep your warrior's respect.

Suddenly there is a blinding explosion in your head and the chain which encircles your neck is being drawn tighter . . . It bites deeply into the flesh of your neck . . . ever tighter!

Your decision was wrong! You try desperately to call out, to warn the others. But that is impossible now. Your blood pounds hard and hot at your temples and you begin to loose consciousness.

You realize then that you too have fallen victim to the dreaded ninja. What will happen to your beloved lord? You will never know . . . for you will sleep forever.

The End

# Other Titles in the Tuttle Library of Martial Arts

## AIKIDO AND THE DYNAMIC SPHERE
*by Adele Westbrook and Oscar Ratti*

> Aikido is a Japanese method of self-defense that can be used against any form of attack and that is also a way of harmonizing all of one's vital powers into an integrated, energy-filled whole.

## BEGINNING QIGONG: CHINESE SECRETS OF FITNESS *by Stephen Kuei and Stephen Comee*

> A straightforward, easy-to-use text on this powerful art of self-healing. Learn the Chinese secrets of health and longevity through these easy and graceful exercises.

## BEYOND THE KNOWN: THE ULTIMATE GOAL OF THE MARTIAL ARTS *by Tri Thong Dang*

> A novel that illustrates one man's quest to find the way of the martial arts. A work that will make you question your motives and goals, and go beyond the dazzle of prizes and awards, beyond the repetition of techniques, and beyond the known—the ultimate goal of the arts.

## BLACK BELT KARATE *by Jordan Roth*

> A no-frills, no-holds-barred handbook on the fundamentals of modern karate. Over 800 techniques and exercises and more than 1,850 photographs reveal the speed and power inherent in properly taught karate.

## COMPLETE TAI-CHI: THE DEFINITIVE GUIDE TO PHYSICAL AND EMOTIONAL SELF-IMPROVEMENT *by Alfred Huang*

> A step-by-step guide to the practice, history, and philosophy of Wu-style Tai-chi. Including unique English translations of original Chinese texts, it is the most complete work on this holistic and spiritual art.

## THE ESSENCE OF OKINAWAN KARATE-DO
*by Shoshin Nagamine*

> "Nagamine's book will awaken in all who read it a new understanding of the Okinawan open-handed martial art."
> —Gordon Warner
> *Kendo 7th dan, renshi*

## ESSENTIAL SHORINJIRYU KARATEDO
*by Masayuki Kukan Hisataka*

A well-rounded guide to this highly innovative and effective ı.ıartial art. Describing preset forms, fighting combinations, and weapons, it is an excellent introduction to this comprehensive fighting system.

## FILIPINO MARTIAL ARTS: CABALES SERRADA ESCRIMA *by Mark V. Wiley*

An excellent introduction to this deadly but graceful Filipino art of armed and unarmed combat. Packed full of information on the techniques, tactics, philosophy, spirituality, and history of the Filipino martial arts, this book is a vital addition to any martial arts library.

## THE HAND IS MY SWORD: A KARATE HANDBOOK
*by Robert A. Trias*

The history, the fundamentals, the basic techniques, and katas are brought to life by over 600 illustrations in this book, which teaches that to master others one must first master oneself.

## HSING-I: CHINESE INTERNAL BOXING
*by Robert W. Smith and Allen Pittman*

A superb introduction to the Chinese art of Hsing-i that both beginners and advanced practitioners can use to probe deeply into the secrets of one of the most complete systems of self-defense yet developed.

## JUDO FORMAL TECHNIQUES
*by Tadao Otaki and Donn F. Draeger*

A comprehensive manual on the basic formal techniques of Kodokan Judo, the *Randori no Kata*, which provide the fundamental training in throwing and grappling that is essential to effective Judo.

## KARATE: THE ART OF "EMPTY-HAND" FIGHTING
*by Hidetaka Nishiyama and Richard C. Brown*

A highly acclaimed, unexcelled treatment of the techniques and principles of karate. Includes over 1,000 easy-to-follow illustrations and a thorough review of the history and organization of the art.

## KARATE BREAKING TECHNIQUES *by Jack Hibbard*

The first book solely on the art and technique of breaking. Over 500 outstanding photographs show clearly how to execute breaks in a simple step-by step manner.

## THE KARATE DOJO: TRADITIONS AND TALES OF A MARTIAL ART *by Peter Urban*

This book discusses in detail the *dojo*, or training hall. Gives anecdotes on the origins and history of karate, as well as on the important role it has played in history.

## KARATE'S HISTORY AND TRADITIONS
*by Bruce A. Haines*

Written by a historian, this book both describes the origins of karate and explains the importance of Zen in the serious study of karate.

## THE NINJA AND THEIR SECRET FIGHTING ART
*by Stephen K. Hayes*

> The ninja were the elusive spies and assassins of feudal Japan. This book explains their lethal system of unarmed combat, unique weapons, and mysterious techniques of stealth.

## NINJA WEAPONS: CHAIN AND SHURIKEN
*by Charles V. Gruzanski*

> The only book on the Masaki-ryu, which uses the "ten-thousand power chain" and *Shuriken-jutsu*, which uses metal projectiles developed to help swordless ninja defeat armed samurai.

## PA-KUA: EIGHT-TRIGRAM BOXING
*by Robert W. Smith and Allen Pittman*

> This book outlines the history and philosophy of the martial art based on the Pa-kua, the eight trigrams of the I-Ching. A definitive guide to this internal Chinese martial art.

## THE SECRETS OF JUDO: A TEXT FOR INSTRUCTORS AND STUDENTS
*by Jiichi Watanabe and Lindy Avakian*

> A fully illustrated text on the major *waza*—includes the most important throws, strangles, and pins. An indispensable introduction to judo and its basics.

## SECRETS OF SHAOLIN TEMPLE BOXING
*edited by Robert W. Smith*

> Abundantly and attractively illustrated, this book presents the essence of Shaolin in three sections—its history, its fundamentals, and its techniques—gleaned from a rare Chinese text.